To my Boy Ellis

Keep making that money.
FReedom ToweR money

GooD

money

P. S
love one

Stedrac

Life In St-Lucia

by

Shedrac Decaille

authorHOUSE®

AuthorHouse™
1663 Liberty Drive, Suite 200
Bloomington, IN 47403
www.authorhouse.com
Phone: 1-800-839-8640

First published by AuthorHouse 7/19/2007

ISBN: 1-4259-0383-5 (dj)
ISBN: 1-4184-2478-1 (sc)
ISBN: 1-4184-2477-3 (ebook)

Printed in the United States of America
Bloomington, Indiana

This book is printed on acid-free paper.

Chapter One
St. Lucia the Beautiful

St. Lucia is a different place than America. When I was on the island I enjoyed myself every morning, thank God. I would go to this tree—in fact two trees. One I read on and the other I used as a bathroom, if you know what I mean. The one tree that I read on was the most comfortable tree (or most comfortable place) that I sat on in St. Lucia. In that tree I learned a lot. For example, I watched birds build their nest. You can learn a lot about life from birds. They work together. I saw the homes of termites on that tree. There were so many of them—hundreds, thousands, millions—but only one leader. Imagine that. They all know their jobs and never complain. I learned a lot in my tree.

It is time to eat and drink, so I am happy about that because it is a different kind of breakfast: coconut water every morning. I mean that cold, sweet, jelly coconut—the kind that quenches your soul. The food is all natural all from the ground, with nothing added or taken away. I mean there are no chemicals; it is all natural. My father loved his fish so much. For two months I ate fish. with my father ,now I love fish just as much as my dad. It is all natural; nothing added and nothing taken away, unlike meat. You never know what you are going to eat. Fish is it. Thanks dad. I haven't seen old man in seventeen years. My mother left my father when I was about sixteen, so I always thought my father was an ignorant and wicked man, so we never spoke for about seventeen years, but my trip changed everything. I didn't know how we were going to get along, but God is on my side.

My father is my father, after seventeen years. It felt so good to see him. Thank God he was alive to see me. We talked and ended our differences. I also haven't seen my grandmother in seventeen years, so what could I say about her but call her a super grandma? She is a 101 years old and still smiling. She has no teeth but such a lovely smile. She is still strong enough to grab you; the children call it the claw. She is the great great-grandmother of my sister's daughter's children, which means she has seen four generations of our family.

Well, I have a lot more to say about my grandmother, but not now. All I can say is she worshiped God from the time I knew her, and that's about thirty something years. God bless her for 101 years and counting. Like the energizer bunny, she is still going and going, so I ask God to bless me like my grandmother (P.S. thank you).

Oh man! It feels good in St. Lucia. The freedom, it is just what it is: freedom. I'm sorry to say I smoke trees. No, I am not sorry to say that. In fact that's one of my pleasures. I have many desires. I smoke in the streets, on the beach, next to the waterfall, in the river, on the rocks, and in the hills. Wherever I wanted to do it, I did it. I was not afraid of the man or the police. I respect the police and it's against the law to smoke trees, but you would have to catch me first and you know where I smoke: in the hills or on the rocks.

It's against the law to drink a beer in the streets of America, so I am programmed not to do so. One day we were working on my store, so I had a little celebration, some food, and some beers. I had to leave to check on my bars for my store: two for windows and one for the door. I didn't realize I had a beer in my hand ,so I was about to hide it, but then I realized I was in St. Lucia, so I threw my hands up like they do in a rap concert, exposing the beer I'm talking about. What's up, what's up, damn! It feels good. It's the simple things that make me happy.

One Sunday about eleven o'clock, I went up a hill and climbed to the top of a tree. Oh boy. Not another tree. What can I say? I love trees. I lived seventeen years in America of concrete and steel. You see, I am an ironworker who lived in Brooklyn, so my life is based around my construction jobs, not around nature, which I have grown to love so much since I been to St. Lucia. Trees were one of the first places that I started to learn about life. Anyway, back to the story. I climb to the top of the tree with my CD player, listening to Bob Marley, one of my heroes. I have many heroes. In fact all my heroes are dead. They all died for what they believed in: smoking and thinking about life. The wind was blowing a little cool air through the leaves. In fact the leaves make the air cool. Sitting on a branch, rocking back and forth in the wind with no one to bug me and no one telling me to get off that tree!

From my branch I could see St. Lucia's yellow-sand beaches, and the water is as blue as the sky on a cloudless day. The view from the top of the tree makes me breathless and it's freeing, so I ask God to give me a piece of paradise.

Life is for the living, and in St. Lucia I taste life and it feels good. I learn to ride a motorbike, which I always wanted to do. I always imagined owning one as a teenager, but my family was so broke that they couldn't pay attention.

Between four and five o'clock every day, I would go running for no reason or because I could. I am not a runner but I am in St. Lucia, and the feeling is upon me to do so, so I run. See what you did, St. Lucia? You gave me life again. I could run freely and didn't have to worry about what neighborhood I could not run through.

My favorite runs are at the airport. The airport is about more then a mile long and it's against the law to cross it. But when I was a child, you could just simply walk across it because there were less flights back then. But now St. Lucia is getting more popular, so there are more flights to the land. I would run one on side of the airport, passing the security house, ignoring the sign that read: "Warning. It is prohibited to cross the airport." I would wait for a minute to see if any planes were coming. If not, I would just run across it to the opposite side and run all the way back down.

Sometimes I would run to a lighthouse, running through some rich neighborhood where no police were there to stop me, but some dogs slowed me down. The lighthouse is on top of the hill overlooking the sea and the airport. What a view. I would stay for about twenty minutes to watch the planes touch down and the fishing boats come in with their catch of the day.

Tired from running and now lying on the sand trying to catch my breath and watching the sunset. I had never paid much attention to a sunset before. Do you know that St. Lucia has a special sunset cruise where tourists pay their money to see the sunset? It is the most beautiful and the most romantic view you will ever see, and it's all made possible by the man, Father God.

I call the beach my bathtub. For seventeen years I was away from it. I missed it so much. It is blue like the sky and warm like a mother's arm. Swimming could I still swim? Yes I could. After seventeen years away from it, I still got it. In fact, I swam better than before because I had missed it so much. I was like a kid in a candy store. I didn't know how to

4

act. I just couldn't make up my mind whether to jump in, run in, dive in, or just walk in nice and slow. All I could remember is that it felt so good against my skin and tasted good too—salty but good.

I tried every swimming method I've seen on TV: the backstroke, front stroke, and the butterfly. You name it, I tried it. Just like I said before, I am the kid in the candy store, so I don't know how to act. I enjoy my water so much.

One day about four o'clock in the afternoon, two guys were going diving, so I asked them, "Can I come with you guys?" So they asked me if I could swim. "But of course!" I said. I guess they thought that seventeen years away from my homeland made me lose my skills. But I am in St. Lucia now and I can do anything. I had never been diving before because I always had a fear of the unknown. On the other hand, I always had a burning desire for it.

So we jumped in the back of the guy's pickup truck and drove off to our destination. On the ride to our diving spot, I kept thinking about all the scary movies I had seen, like Jaws. Now my negative thinking and my fear of the unknown had me nervous. But we are there. There was no turning back for me now, to tell you the truth. I was a little scared but very anxious.

The water is a little bit rough but inviting, so we jump on in. One guy has the fishing spear gun. The other has a bag so they can put the fish into it. And I am the curious one, the bystander. After a couple of swallows of seawater and almost drowning, my confidence started coming back. Now I am diving well—not that good, but well enough to keep my mouth closed. It felt like I was in a big giant aquarium. *Oh man! I am actually swimming with the fishes*, I thought. I could see all kinds of fish: all shapes, colors, and all different sizes.

The guy with the gun was good. He could go down for about a minute and come up with a fish on the end of his spear. Once in a while he would miss, but not that often. Whenever he came up, the other guy would take the fish off his spear to put in the bag. I watched that for a while and the next time he came up, I grabbed the fish off the spear to put in the bag. I felt like the cameraman on National Geographic. I had to jump in; I could not help myself. So every time he came up I would take a fish off his spear.

Now I am looking around and full of joy because I am diving. Then all of a sudden I see something: a sea egg, one of my favorite kinds of raw seafood. When I was a young boy, we used to go looking for sea eggs close to the rocks. There are two types of sea eggs: the black one and the white one. The black one is the dangerous one. It looks like a ball covered in spikes. If you step on the black one, some of the spikes will be release into your feet, and one of the ways you can get those spikes out is someone urinating on your feet. We learn that from the old people, and it works.

But it is the white one I am after. You can break the shell and eat the inside of the white one. Actually it's the eggs on the inside we ate. It is yellow and sweet, so we eat it right away and it tastes good. The correct name for it is *sea urchin*. I saw it, but the guy with the bag saw it too. Guess who got there first? You are right: me. I didn't know how far or deep the egg was, so we both went down together. I grabbed the egg right off his fingertips. He looked at me like I was crazy. *You're damn right I am crazy!* I rushed back to the surface out of breath but I got the egg.

I decided to venture out on my own, exploring the bottom of St. Lucia's beautiful blue waters, watching the fish hide themselves between the beautiful island coral reefs. My eyes have seen the natural beauty of God's creation. I looked around some more until I found two more sea eggs and then looked around for my guys. They were at least a hundred feet away from me, so I swam back to them and put my eggs in the bag.

We spent about three hours in the water. Then I started getting cold. The sun started going down, so it is getting a little dark. It was dark and I was still in the water watching another beautiful Caribbean sunset. After my enjoyment of the sun, we started swimming toward the shore. The first thing I did was grab the sea eggs out of the bag. I broke the first one but nothing was in it, so I broke open the second one and the same thing happened. Then I broke open the third one. I kept my fingers crossed and hoped for the sweet yellow egg on the inside, but the same thing happened to me again. Nevertheless, I enjoyed myself.

The next day the guys made a big meal from their catch and save me a big fat plate. The two guys that took me diving also lived with five more guys in the same house. They all had come from the countryside looking for work, so they moved to the city to make a better living. The city is called Castries. That's the capital of beautiful St. Lucia.

One Saturday I was going to the beach to read. I didn't really want to go, because I did it every Saturday. I wanted to do something different, so on my way to the beach I meet two of those country guys going somewhere. So I asked them,

"Where are you guys going?" They told me they were going fishing, so I asked them if I could come.

"Why not?" they answered.

"We are going river fishing in the country," one said to me, "but they are going without any fishing poles or fishing net, just the gasses."

We stopped and waited for two more guys who were also from the countryside. After about an hour of waiting, they came. We took a transport to the country, where the guys used to live. We made a stop at one of the guy's parents' house so they could change clothes. I was still wondering what kind of fishing they could possibly do without fishing poles or nets. Then one of the guys came out with a long nail. It was not exactly a nail, but that's the only way I can describe it. It was about three feet long with an elastic band on one end, and the other end was a sharp as a nail.

I have a feeling I am not going to enjoy myself in that river, because it's probably dirty and stinky, I thought. *A place where people dump whatever they want.* When we got there my mouth dropped to the ground. I couldn't believe my eyes. *Oh man! St. Lucia has some whitewater rivers. The water is crystal clear and the people are friendly toward me.*

My excitement got the best of me. *Look at all those big rocks*, I thought. The water is flowing all around the big rock and the little ones too. It looks like the rocks are directing the water. Water cannot go through rocks, so the rocks change the direction of the water. It also looks like the rocks are being used by the river, because it traps all the garbage so the water can flow crystal clear.

I always, always say to myself, *If I ever go back to my country I will smoke a fat joint on a big rock by the river.* After seventeen years, guess what I am doing right now? Smoking one on that big rock I always dream about.

I started noticing the guys pushing their hands under the rocks like they were looking for something. But what? We kept on walking upstream in the water. I had on my sandals and was enjoying the water flowing between my toes. I hoped the water cleaned them well, because my wife always complains about my stinky toes.

8

The guys kept on pushing their hands under more rocks. Then one of them jumped up and grabbed the long nail and the glasses. He went back down under the rock and came up with a crayfish on the end of the nail. A crayfish is the cousin of the shrimp and lobster family with claws. And it can grow to be twice the size of jumbo shrimp, one of my favorite foods.

The nail is used as a fishing gun. You put the elastic between your two fingers, the thumb and the pointer finger, then pull and release. Guess who had to carry the crayfish? Me. You are right again. I am the curious bystander who always has to get into something.

I carried the crayfish on a long, skinny stick with a hook on one end so that the crayfish wouldn't fall off. One of the guys would push the stick through the tail of the crayfish one by one, like a shish-kabob stick. I finally realize what they are doing. They are crayfish diving. Tha stupid!

The flowing of the water brings down the crayfish so the crayfish have to find a place to hide and under a rock is the best place for them. The river also brings down other things, like crab, eel, and all kinds of fish. Now, guess where they all hide. That's right: under those rocks.

I would have to be brave enough to put my hands under those rocks because of the crabs and eels, but I am not. One of the guys is very brave. They would call him when any hole looked dark and dangerous. He do not need any gun—just his bare hands. There is no place too dark or scary for him to try. He would push his hands under any rock. Remember now, anything could be under those rocks. One time that same guy pushed his hand under a rock and came up with two crayfish in one hand. Everyone freaked out because that was the first time that had ever happened to them.

Oh baby! I am enjoying myself with strangers and no one is treating me strangely. Nobody else can tell if I am a foreigner, because I blend in so well with the country boys. The river is a beautiful place to go to.

The river is flowing smoothly, so the rocks are being washed by the water. The birds are singing. The trees are bent over on both sides of the river, so they covered the sides like an umbrella, but the bright sun could still shine directly in the middle of the river, reflecting off the crystal-clear water, making it look like the reflection of a mirror. Bling, Bling.

I am seeing different things. Some people are washing their clothes, and others are just taking a bath in that clean, natural mountain water. The people I like the most are the ones who are cooking food. I think they call that a river picnic. Oh how I wish my wife and kids were invited to that picnic. We would only have to bring the cooking pot and some matches. The river produces all kinds of fruit and ground foods, and if you know your herbs, the river provided them too. And as for the meat, you could look for crayfish, crabs, fish, and eels.

We are still traveling up the river. So far the others had caught about twenty of them and a good-sized fish. I am carrying the crayfish on the shish-kabob stick, and sometimes I would rest it against my leg, forgetting that the crayfish have claws. Once in a while I would feel a pinch on my side. They take about an hour to die. Now I am curious but not brave enough to try it.

I wanted to take a bath in that crystal-clear water, but the guys told me they were taking me to a special place. We keep on walking upstream and the water still felt good going through my toes. It took us about a half hour more before we got to that special place. It was a big hole in the middle of the river—like a small swimming pool but really deep.

The guys put their stuff down and climbed to the top of the rock and jumped in. I was not too sure about that so I walked in. The guys wanted to know who could touch the bottom of the pool. They all touched it. I could not remember if I touched it our not, but I was taking a bath in crystal-clear Poland spring water, on the island of beautiful St. Lucia.

I came out of the pool and put on the glasses and decided to look for crayfish on my own. I never put my hands under any rocks, because I am afraid of what an eel could do to my fingers. An eel is a snake-like creature with teeth that are as sharp as a blade. With one strike it could cut off your finger or leave a nasty, nasty cut. I did move a couple of rocks to see what was under them, but never found anything. I am enjoying my Saturday— the Sabbath, the Lord's Day.

I finally decide to climb to the top of the rock, where the guys were jumping from. There is a small waterfall on the top of the big one that falls into the pool below. From where I am standing it looks like the force of the water created the pool below. Water is also nature's most precious gift. You can survive without money but you cannot live without water, so you see, there is more to life than money.

After about an hour they decided to head back down the river. Going back down is a lot different than coming up. The guys are running down the river—not in the water but on the side of the river.

I thought they forgot that I am a foreigner, because they are running very fast down stream. There aren't any roads, so you must be good to keep up with those country boys with no shoes on their feet. After such a long time away, I still got it. The road is an obstacle course. There are fallen trees, big rocks, slippery roots, and waterholes. So you must have skills to jump from rock to rock, ducking under the falling trees and jumping over the waterholes without missing a beat. Once in a while the guys would look back to see if I was still keeping up with them. "Hey guys I am still here," I said. I thanked God for this vacation.

Halfway down, we stopped next to an orange tree, where the riverbanks are filled with fruit. This is how those guys pick oranges, they don't climb the trees. They throw stones at the oranges. You should know me by now; I had to join in. I threw a couple of stones before I knocked an orange down. My throwing became better and better, and soon I had enough to eat. I used the baseball technique: look, aim, and fire. That's also one of the ways they pick mangos and coconuts. I believe if you want a good pitcher, you should go to St. Lucia first. Some team could use the help. Those were some of the sweetest oranges I ever tasted, and I am not just saying that because I was in St. Lucia. The trees are naturally grown. There is no help from scientists, only Mother Nature.

After our orange break, we kept on running down the river until we reached the guy's parent's house. I'd never had crayfish before, so I was thinking that soon it would be time to eat. But the guys came out all dressed up and talking about it is time to head back home.

We get on the transport that heads to the city. On my ride home I am thinking those guys are greedy for not sharing with me. Now mentally I am vexed after I had worked so hard carrying those crayfish. They could have at least given me about four. Anyway, we got home and some of the night I was still thinking about that. The next day, to my surprise, my friends who I had thought so badly about had a big fat plate waiting on me. I got ate down on that plate like there was no tomorrow. I almost licked the plate. It just wasn't enough for me. It was cooked country style; everything was in one pot, like gumbo. I liked those seven guys. They treated me very well.

Chapter Two
Hidden Paradise

Round and round the island I go. What will I see? Nobody knows. One day my cousin and his friend decided to take me around St. Lucia to see the island's beauty. First we drove through the marketplace, and what a beautiful place it was to see on our way to the countryside.

It didn't take me long to realize the beauty of the island. We drove up this mountain. St. Lucia has lots of mountains, so people could get a better picture of the island's beauty. I kept noticing people selling things on the sides of the mountain or at the viewpoint, a place where tourists would stop to admirer the island's beauty.

On that mountaintop you will get a bird's eye view of the ocean. St. Lucia's ocean is as blue as the sky on certain days, if there aren't any clouds in the sky. I could see three different shades of blue in the sea: royal blue, sky blue, and baby blue. Television can't give you a good picture of it. You have to see it yourself. Wow.

There is also the beauty of the trees from that same spot. You can see the chicken hawks gliding over the treetops. The wind is moving the tops of the trees back and forth, like a mother rocks her baby to sleep. Oh how I wish I were one of those chicken hawks standing on that mountaintop. I would spread my wings and glide over the treetops and dive straight into that cool baby blue water.

After I got a hold on my imagination, we kept on driving. It didn't take me long to notice the banana trees—I mean acres and acres of banana and coconut trees. Bananas are one of St. Lucia's biggest exports and half of our diet. It didn't take long to see the beauty of the countryside.

The island has many famous sites, and one of the most famous ones is called the Pitons. It is the two most beautiful mountains side by side, like a pair of silicone breasts pointing to the sky, but one is bigger then the other. The mountains got their name from the French because the island was controlled by them, but then came the British. Those two colonial powers fought fourteen times for sweet St-Lucia , British won seven and the French won seven . I can see what they were fighting for: hidden paradise. Now St. Lucia is an independent island.

The big one is called go Piton, and the little one is called pity Piton, which means big mountain and little mountain. The mountain are so much a part of the island that they have named a beer after them. It is called Piton. The mountain made its first guest appearance in the movie *Superman II.* It happened when Superman was about to propose to Lois Lane. He took her to a piece of his planet Krypton, and then he flew all the way to a beautiful island called St. Lucia, just to get her a special rose. And in the background was a beautiful shot of those two mountains side by side, pointing to the sky.

In my soul, St. Lucia is life, and you know life is for the living. We kept on driving with the wind blowing through the car and the radio playing some good old-time reggae that I haven't heard in a long time. The music makes me move my head back and forth, moving and thinking about life in St. Lucia, hoping this never ends.

My cousin seemed to know every back road and shortcut there is, even the ones behind God's back; if you know what I mean. I enjoy driving through those back roads, because I get to see a whole lot more than the average sightseer. We are driving through the heart of the country, where the beauty stays beautiful.

I saw a tree that I haven't seen in seventeen years. It's called a coco tree. I told my cousin to pull the car over and I jumped out to climb one of those coco trees and pick two pieces of fruit. The fruit is called the coco fruit and this is how you eat it. First you break the shell and suck on the seeds on the inside, but remember, don't swallow the seeds. The seeds are covered with a white creamy sweet stuff that melts in your mouth and doesn't melt in your hands. The seeds are very useful and the people on the island would put the seeds in the sun to dry and then crush the seeds into coco sticks. The sticks are used to make coco tea or rich hot chocolate, one of the best and richest teas on the island, and I brought some home.

They are taking me to see a volcano, but I call it the living power of God. It's a living volcano and you can see the inside of it bubbling. Besides the pitons, the volcano is one of the land's biggest tourist attractions. People from all over the world come to see it, even scientists. I myself had never seen a volcano before, so when we got there I noticed a long line to get into the park to see the living volcano. It only cost one dollar to get in, but we snuck in. That's just the ghetto in me.

We walk down a small hill into the river, and the water is as black as tar and smells like God knows what. I see people taking a bath in that water, so I ask my cousin how they can do that. He told me that dirty water is the water from the volcano and the old people say it is good for the skin. It must be true because there is a white woman laying in that water with a big smile on her face. He also told me that people drink the water to clean their insides. After seventeen years of hamburgers and hotdogs, I put my two hands together and drank two handfuls of dirty water. It tasted like water mix with sand and it was very warm.

So I told myself the next time I came to St. Lucia I would take a bath in that dirty warm water with a big smile on my face, like that white woman.

We climbed to the other side to get a better view of the volcano. I was actually standing about fifty feet from the volcano, and I could see the insides boiling like a pot. I could smell it but I cannot remember how it smelled. I could also feel the heat coming from it and could see the steam rising to the sky. There are all kinds of people here, from all nations, enjoying the view. I noticed a native guy chipping pieces of the volcanic rock to sell to the foreigners as souvenirs.

Do you know that's probably, maybe, the only volcano in the world where people like you and me can get so close to it? Scientists from all over world come down to study it. They are trying to figure out ways to use all the natural energy to help the country. That's why I call it the living power of God. The only other word that can describe is *breathless*.

After being mesmerized by God's beauty, we decided to walk over to the refreshment stand. I told them they could have what ever they wanted, and you know when it's free you can eat twice as much. But I do not mind, because I was enjoying myself. I had some fried fish and fried dumplings with a nice cold glass of homemade juice, and I ate till my belly was full. I sat down under a little shady tree to relax for a couple of minutes, and then my mind started to run wild about my life and about St. Lucia.

I was born on this beautiful island but never knew about its hidden beauty. There are white people walking around the island with no troubles on their minds. It looks like they just got up one morning, packed a small bag, and jumped on the first plane straight to the island called St. Lucia, or may I say, paradise.

Everybody needs a vacation or a little time away to clear his or her mind, especially black skin people. After working so hard in America, working paycheck to paycheck and paying bills, it looked like I would never get a break in life. But sometimes in life you have to be brave enough to take a chance on the things you want in life. You never know. The vacation changed my whole life. Before, I was angry and frustrated, but now I finally understand why white folks take a family vacation every year. It releases stress.

You don't want to be sixty-five years old and regret not taking that vacation. Maybe that one vacation could have changed your whole life. I know it can because it changed mine. Always remember you only have one life to live, so live life while you still have it and thank God for this book. I hope you are enjoying my company.

My cousins called me about four or five times before I stopped daydreaming. We jumped back into the car and drove off. I kept on looking back at the volcano and asked myself, "Am I dreaming or am I on vacation?" *No, I am not dreaming,* I thought. *I am on my first vacation and I hope it is not my last.*

We drove to our next destination, the waterfall. When we got there the place was closed. Actually there was a small gate made out of bamboo sticks and a piece of rope that suggested the place was closed. So we untied the rope and headed on in.

We walk past a small hut that's made out of straw and bamboo sticks and walk down some steps that have been carved into the mountainside.

They lead to the waterfall. It is not Niagara Falls, but to me it is just as beautiful.

I take my clothes off and jump into water. After a hot, and one of my most exciting days I had on my vacation. The cool, refreshing water feels good against my body. I climb to the top of the waterfall and sit directly under the water. It feels like the Lord is pouring his showers of blessings upon my head. I bend my head forward to let the water massage my neck. You couldn't pay for a better massage. After ten minutes with my favorite masseur, I got up and jumped into the pool below me. When I came up for air my whole life changed. There was no one else around, so I said to my cousins, "If I can't come back to St. Lucia, then all my hopes and dreams are dead."

This is the first time I ever enjoyed life so much, and it makes me feel like a runaway slave who has just won his freedom papers, so you know I am making big splashes in the water. The rising of the sun and the crowing of the rooster wake me up every morning, so no alarm clock is needed. When the sun rises, I rise also, because every day in St. Lucia brings a different adventure, so I never know what will happen to me. But it will be a good day after all.

I have no one telling me what to do and no laws restricting me from going where I wanna go or doing what I wanna do. Life is all I have and life is what I wanna know about. Also, life is what you make it, and in St. Lucia I enjoy it for what it's worth. So no matter what happens to me from now on, my experience lives on forever.

I look forward to the greetings of the people every morning because they bring joy to my soul. I have never met so many people who look forward to seeing me every day, and my feeling is also the same. They say home is where your heart is, but I say, "Home is where someone welcomes you with open arms."

I am intoxicated from the beauty and friendliness of the island. The things I did and the things I saw changed my life for good.

I swam around in natural waters and smiled to myself. I almost forgot that we snuck into the place, and then from the mountaintop we heard a voice calling out to us, "Yo, you, what is going on?" My cousin answered, "Rastamon, Rastamon, we will take care of you when we come up." So he replied "okay."

Then my cousin told me that the government gave the Rastamon and his partner that particular piece of land with the waterfall, as long as they could take care of the place. So they had built a fence and carved steps into the mountainside for better access to the waterfall. They had also built a small freshwater pond with all kinds of freshwater fish. To my eyes the place looked very clean and the grass looked properly groomed. This particular waterfall is the kind of place where you would take your wife or someone special. It's romantic and almost private. Not too many people go to it.

We stayed for another ten minutes; then we headed upstairs. On my way up I asked my cousin how much should I give the Rastamon. He replied, "Give him whatever you have." All I had was about twenty dollars change, so he answered "that's cool." When we got to the hut, that's where the Rastamon was waiting for us with a big fat joint in his hand. I told him that we didn't mean any disrespect by entering his place like that. He looked at me and smiled, so I gave him the twenty I had. He asked me where I was from, so I said Brooklyn. No matter where you are, Brooklyn is always in the house or the hut.

19

We kept on talking about the country and the families. Then he passed me the joint—not any joint, but a big fat Rastamon joint. It was the kind you would have to use all five fingers to hold onto. I took three good pulls and passed it. He took a couple of puffs and passed it back to me but I refused. Most people smoke trees to forget about their problems, but I smoke trees to help me figure out my problems.

After our friendly conversation, we all head to the bamboo gate. When we got to the gate there was a blue pickup truck waiting for the Rastamon. He jumped on the back of that pickup truck, sat down, and rolled up another fat one. He lit up and drove off into the sunset. We also jumped in our car and drove off into that same sunset. On my ride home, I kept on thinking about my life in America. America is a place of hopes and dreams, but on the other hand it can be your worst nightmare, I know.

I came to United States for one reason only. That is to make a better living for me and my family. Since the time I came to this country, I have been working construction and trying to pay my bills on time. Sometimes life doesn't always go as planned, so I kept on praying and praying to the Father to show me a better way. He told me, "Laziness will make you poor, but hard work and a good plan will make you rich and secure."

After fifteen years of working so hard with no plan, I couldn't accomplish anything with my life. Now because of my prayer to God I have a plan, and it is to work hard for myself and enjoy my one life wherever I go. I have a lot more to say about my life, but you have to promise me you will keep on reading; cross your fingers and hope to die.

All night long I keep on thinking about the day I had. My mother and I left the island when I was sixteen, so I never really enjoyed the island's beauty. I was lucky enough to find my second love, which is St. Lucia. You should know my first one by now. I hate to repeat myself over and over again, but I must. St. Lucia put the fire of life in me, so now my new life has a meaning and a purpose, and the meaning is to share my love with you and help you with some words of encouragement.

Chapter Three
Boat Ride

I always fantasize about owning a boat before I die, because to me a boat symbolizes freedom. I have never been on a boat before, but I always imagine myself out in the open blue sea with no one around to bug me—just the cool, fresh ocean air and the songs of the waves hitting against my boat.

One day a friend invited me on a boat ride that went into the island's countryside. This would be my first time, so I could not refuse it. He brought me a ticket, so off we went. When we got to the harbor, we waited for about an hour or more. You know what? It doesn't matter where you go, black folks are always late.

Then out of the clear blue sea, I heard something sweet: the songs of the freedom boat playing my wife's favorite calypso song—the kind that forces me to dance. We all started entering the boat and the guys were checking out the fine ladies, thinking to themselves, "I would like to grind on this one all night long to this sweet calypso music."

I got on the boat, walked straight to the front, and sat down at the nose of the boat with my feet hanging over the water. We waited for another half hour to make sure everything was put on board, like the foods, the drinks, and (don't forget) the fine ladies.

Our boat is a sailboat: nice and flat with a lot of room to get your freak on. And it was made for partying. After everything was on board, I started my first boat ride, and this one was going around the island—not the whole island, but most of it. Now I could enjoy St. Lucia from a different view, or the ocean's view.

Cutting through that baby blue water with my feet dangling over the boat, once in a while a nice-sized wave would make the boat take a nosedive, causing that blue saltwater to splash all over my body. This may not be exciting to you, but this was my first vacation and I was enjoying every moment of it. I could die tomorrow, but today saltwater is all over me.

People are starting to drink and are associating and waiting for the first dancer to hit the floor. And I am in front, checking out the beautiful mountains of St. Lucia and the lovely hotels alongside the seashore. I could see some of the most spectacular houses ever built on top of those mountains.

You could see a vision of the owner coming out early every morning with coffee in his or her hands and that nice, cool, gentle sea breeze blowing all over his or her body—the kind of breeze that makes you hug yourself.

After being fascinated by the beautiful scenery of that vision, I turn my attention back to the party. Some people are on the floor doing their thing, so the place is a little more lively now.

St. Lucia is a bilingual island because of the French and the British. The island got its independence, I think, in 1979 from the British, and the two different languages we speak are English and Creole.

I decided to walk around and mingle with the crowd a little bit. Then I walked to the back of the boat with my camera. There are many different kinds of boat and yachts carrying people to enjoying this tropical breeze of St. Lucia. All the yachts carry flags so you can tell what country they are from. I see the Italian flag, the English flag, Canadian flag, and some flags

I can't recognize. Then everyone turns their attention to this one yacht with the American icon on it. And if you know America: bigger is better. I took a couple of pictures of the yachts and boats, especially the American boat. The other boaters also took pictures of our party boat.

Happiness is written all over my face and sadness is nowhere to be found. The place is getting hotter and hotter, so the men are moving a little closer to the ladies, who are putting on a show for the men. "Food will be served in ten minutes," someone shouts from the crowd. I couldn't wait that long. Plus I knew what they would be serving; it was my island's national dish. They may not admit it, but they all grew up on it.

I did not want to be the first one in line, because it might have show my greediness, so I took a slow walk over. When I got there five people were already in line for their favorite island food. It was green banana and codfish, or like we St. Lucians like to call it, green fig and salt-fish. Mm, good. It may not sound like an exotic food, but cook with the right amount of oil and seasoning and we St. Lucian's cannot resist our national dish.

I got my plate and told myself, *I must eat this fast so I can get back in line for a second plate.* It was an all-inclusive boat ride, so you could eat as much as you wanted and drink as much as you could handle. So I got my second plate, headed to the back, sat down, and tried to stuff my belly as much as I could.

Full to the brim with my favorite island food and was unable to move. My mind started wandering. St. Lucia, home of yellow-sand beaches and miles of beautiful blue water (and don't forget the mountains in the background), was the perfect picture at sunset.

I thank God for those mountains. When I was about nine years old, I remember the island got hit hard by a hurricane that destroyed almost half the country. The other half was saved because of our big mountains. The houses that were built on the top of those mountains were destroyed, but the house that was built at the foot of those mountains or the middle of it was safe. Our house was built in the middle, so we were safe. But as for the house that was built on top of our hill, the next day the owner came looking for his roof in my father's yard. I love to see those mountains. They protect lovely St. Lucia like the sea protects its secrets. And while I'm thinking about mountains, our boat was approaching our two famous mountains standing side by side like the king and queen of mountains.

Our boat is about to make its first stop, so we are pulling into the dock. This is one of the places where party boats and some small taxi boats carrying foreigners make their stop.

I notice the kids running and diving off the pier like they are in a competition. In fact, those kids are working and surviving. St. Lucia is a sweet place but not too many jobs are available, so you much find a way to make some money.

Those kids are diving for change, and it does not matter how far you throw your money; the kids will run and jump off the pier and come up with the money before it can touch the bottom. Those kids are about eight to sixteen years old, and you should know me by now; I decided to join in on the throwing. So I threw a coin dollar as far as I could. Before my hand came back to my side, some kid came up with the coin. I threw coins on the left side of the boat, on the right side, and anywhere I thought they could get them. Those kids deserved all the coins they collected, so I loved throwing my money around.

It would be an hour before we continued this boat ride, so that gave me enough time to check out this part of St. Lucia: the countryside.

This is the south part of the island, where the people speak Creole. I cannot speak too much of it myself, but I can understand most of it. I was born in the capital of St. Lucia, which is Castries, and my parents didn't teach us Creole, because they wanted us to learn English alone. Back then people who spoke only Creole were considered ignorant or stupid country bumpkins.

We walk around the town and marketplace to see what's going on. Today is Sunday, so not too many people are out selling in those two places. One of the guys told me that he has a friend in this town, so we should go and check him out. When we got there, there he was sitting on a chair on the sidewalk or in the streets. Most of the streets do not have sidewalks. He was sitting with a big weed branch in his hand, grooming it like his pet. He didn't look worried about the police or the people who walked past him.

He took us to the back of his house overlooking the sea. It looked right at the fisherman's port. Then he passed me a joint—not a little one, but a West Indian one. It was the kind that brother Bob would be proud of.

Being a foreigner has its advantages, especially when they know you are an American. They believe that if you come from America you have money because America's streets are paved with gold. So I use my Yankee accent, and everyone gives me good service. If you feel like you are not getting the love that you deserve, an island vacation will be very nice for you. About 90 percent of the people I met were friendly to me. Most of the people were broke or very broke, but I had never met so many poor people who were willing to share their food with me. Yes, this is an island where people treat you like people. I wouldn't say everything is good, but you would hear 'good morning" a couple of times.

One day I heard a kid talking to a lady on the sidewalk. By the slang he used I could tell that he was from Brooklyn. She said to him, "You are leaving for America tomorrow." By the expression on his face you could tell that he didn't want to leave paradise, and I know why. He knew that he would never get the love and freedom that he received on the island in America.

We stay in his backyard for a while, enjoying the cool Sunday breeze blowing through the trees. I sat directly under a shady tree so I could feel the full effect of my outside air conditioning.

After my meditation from my Bob Marley joint, we said goodbye and walked back to our party boat. When we got there we had to wait a little while longer to make sure everyone got on the right boat. There are two other boats parked along side of us, and they are exactly the same.

There will be a dance contest in about twenty minutes, and after that we will be going to a secluded beach. Music is playing, people are drinking, and the freaks cannot wait for the contest to begin. The winners will receive a bottle of champagne and the title "freak of the week."

Now the contest is on. Calypso music mixes with West Indian rum makes a person forget about his or her shame. I was right about the winners; they were very freaky, and it never got out of hand. The one girl who won the contest danced on the floor with her legs crossed behind her neck and in many more seductive positions.

After the contest, she became the hottest girl in the place. Every man was after her, wondering if she could really do that behind closed doors. I know men, and some men are dogs; wuf, wuf.

This is not one of St. Lucia's many yellow-sand beaches. This one has black sand and it's rare and beautiful. You can see the sparkling in the black sand. It's like stolen treasure in a pirate's eyes; it sparkles.

I took this time to work on my physical condition by jogging up and down the black-sand beach and doing ten pushups every time I went back and fourth. I am trying to look good for my wife with my own island workout. Some days I would take an early morning run, and in the evening I try to play soccer to build up my stamina. Not only women have to look good for their men, but men also have to look good for their mates.

I thought if I could just lose my stomach and build a little bit of muscle, maybe she would love her new and improved man dingo. I hurt my neck by doing too many pushups, so I had to stop my island workout, but I did manage to lose some weight.

There are not too many fat people or overweight children on the island and I know why. I couldn't find any of my favorite fast food restaurants like in Brooklyn. So I had to eat what they ate: foods from the garden and fresh fish from the fisherman's net. Not too many calories are in those foods, so I am getting skinner.

Black sand between my toes, I am enjoying my one life, just like is suppose. This has been an all-day boat ride, but all good things come to an end. The blowing of the boat horn lets everybody know it's time to leave. Soon the sun will be setting, so I will sit back, relax, and take in another beautiful sunset. The music is hitting hard and the people are getting comfortable with each other, so a lot of grinding is taking place. The girl who won the contest is the most sought-out person in the place. The men are on fire and her dancing style is what they desire.

Dancing to calypso music is like having dry sex. I remember my first calypso dance. I was about thirteen years old and I had never been stimulated by a girl before (only by my hands).

We danced in a corner against the wall. The minute she held me my flagpole rose up. Now I was trying to push her off me just a little bit so I could fix my flagpole, because it is in the wrong place and I knew that she could feel the pole. Every time I got a little space between us, I would try to tuck it in between my legs, but it always popped back up. I was loving it but was embarrassed at the same time. I hoped she was not thinking, "You nasty little boy," but every time I stepped back to fix it, she would hold me a little tighter. Let me tell you a little secret. When I grew up I never wore any underwear when I went out to parties, because I wanted women to feel it, and sometimes a woman would come home with me.

Chapter Four
My Father's House

After the boat ride I went home and thanked the Almighty God for such a sweet time in my life. I lay on my back in my small room with my window open so I could gaze at the moon and stars. It is not a full moon tonight, but a full moon in St. Lucia is really a full moon. It is perfect in all its roundness. It is the light of the world.

Once it was a full-moon night and I wanted to enjoy the light of the moon shining on me. So I rolled a nice small joint and walked up the hill in the back of my father's house and sat on the grass to mellow myself out.

Beauty is in the eyes of the beholder. I didn't see the man in the moon or the cow that jumped over the moon. What I did see was the eye of God. I remember growing up as a child, I used to try to hide myself from the moon because it just kept on following me wherever I went. I used to run as fast as I could so I could see if I could lose it, but whenever I looked up, there it was, right over my head. It didn't matter how fast I ran or where I hid; that faithful moon was always there.

In those days growing up on the island, not too many streetlights were placed in all areas around the island. So growing up without shoes and streetlights made a lot of island people tell stories about their big toes.

My father uses the moon to plant his food. He and the old-time islanders believe that planting certain foods on a full-moon night almost guarantees a full harvest. I like the way my father lives on foods from his land and fish from the sea. He plants all kinds of ground foods on his land, like white and yellow yam, plantain trees, and a whole lot of banana trees. He has a lot more ground food, but I cannot remember their names. He also plants different kinds of peas and seasoning for the food he feeds me every night.

On this small piece of land he owns, there are also two big avocado trees and one big bread-fruit tree. He sells the breadfruit to his neighbors or anyone who wants to buy it. That is how he makes his little money, so some Saturdays he takes whatever he can from the earth to sell at the marketplace.

St. Lucia has two marketplaces. One is in the south and the other is in the capital, which is Castries, and that's where my father lives. On Saturdays, which are big business days, the people from the south bring to our town all the kinds of foods the island produces. If you can't find it on Saturday, we do not grow it on the island.

They lay a blanket on the ground and put all their foods on it so you can see what they are selling. Some of them also have small tables so they can put their more gentle foods on them, like the seasonings and the many different kinds of bush medicine.

The old people know which seasonings to cook with and which ones to take for painful bellyaches. There are so many people selling and buying at the same time that there is hardly any room to walk around. So you have to watch your step because you might step on some woman's tomatoes, and you don't want that drama on your vacation. There are mostly women selling at the marketplace, and a few men sell the sweetest jelly coconut water.

Every morning when I get a chance to go downtown, I always stop to have one of those sweet coconut water drinks. They are not sweet like candy, but their sweetness sweetens your soul. Whenever you go to my island, who me, yes you, make sure you ask the guy for a sweet jelly coconut water. It is better in the morning.

There are foreigners with their cameras taking pictures of women and their foods at the marketplace. Some of the women do not like that, so they hide their faces. One time I paid a woman a dollar for her picture. (They do not want you to take their pictures for free.) The selling of those foods takes place on the outside of the marketplace, but the inside is a whole lot different. This the place that sells the arts and crafts of St. Lucia—the beauty of the island captured on T-shirts, pictures, and posters. I had to go in so I could find out what to buy for my wife and kids before I came back to America.

There are all kinds of arts and crafts made out of coconut branches, like hats made out of leaves of branches woven together until they become a hat. Big brooms, little brooms, and also dusters are made from the same coconut leaves. The coconut itself can be shaped into anything the artist wants, from a boat, to a pair of lovebirds, which are my favorites. There are many more different kinds of arts and island clothing in that same place.

I could see a white couple wearing their island clothes and Rastamon hats with the dreads sewn into it, so it looked like they actually had dreads. I find this very amusing, but they do not care, because they are enjoying their beautiful island vacation.

The government spent some money fixing up the marketplace. I remember as a child that part of the market used to be a slaughterhouse for pigs and cows. Some Friday nights, my friends and I used to go and watch the cows and the pigs get their heads blown off. Two guys pull the cows in and one guy with the shotgun, resting it on the cow's head, pulls the trigger, and we love to see the cows fall to the ground. Now, it is just beautiful.

You could also eat in the same marketplace. There are many small booth restaurants with all our island foods cooked by the local people, not by some fancy hotel, so you could taste the different flavors of St. Lucia, and she tastes good.

Besides my father's house, this is my second breakfast place. Some mornings after my coconut water, I would come to this place and order myself a big bowl of fish broth soup. This is the right food in the morning, besides coconut water. It can give you the vitamins and natural minerals your body needs for a long and hot day on the island. I don't like to be late for that, because so many people order the same thing before they go to work. It's the only food that there is never enough of for all the morning costumers. Fish broth is the sauce of the island.

With the money he made from selling whatever he sold, my father bought the necessities of life. Saturday is also the day he mingles and drinks with his few friends. He owns a couple of hens and roosters, better known as local fowls. He always buys coconuts and some special chicken feed for his favorite friends. He also has a dog named Roger. It's a coward, but it keeps him company.

I notice his chickens always gathering around his front door every morning and evening between five and six o'clock. That's when he feeds them, but today he is going to be a little late, so the chickens will have to wait. They will not leave until he feeds them, so fights always breaks out, especially when all the roosters are in one place at the same time.

Every morning when my father wakes up, he yells out his window, "AAAAAA" to his neighbor and waits for about ten seconds. And if she does not answer, he yells again, "AAAAAA." And then she answers. Some mornings when she gets up first, she says the same thing: "AAAAAA," and waits for his answer. I lie on my bed every morning and listen to them calling each other. I always imagine that one day one of them will call the other and there will be no answer from the other. I always think about that when lying in my bed. But for now, it is good to have a friend that wakes you up every morning.

After their spirits are satisfied with an answer, off my father goes to his kitchen, where his friends are waiting on the outside to be fed. This is something else I also think about when I am lying in my bed. One morning his chickens will be waiting in vain for him. Do you think they will know when he's gone? He fixes some ground coconut mix with some chicken feed to serve to his friends. After that my father spends most of his day on his small piece of land, picking and planting in his own garden. Tonight we have no meat for our dinner, so we have to wait until five or six o'clock. That's when the chickens come home to eat and sleep. He stands in the yard, drops the chicken feed around his feet, and waits for the one he wants to cook tonight. He reaches down and snatches it by the neck, so tonight we are having Bobber the rooster mixed with rice and peas.

After seventeen years, my father and I now talk and laugh as long-lost friends. Whenever we talk, he always tells me about the two things a man needs in the world; one is his house and the other is his own piece of land. Without that a man is not a man, because on the island those two things are your greatest possessions: your house and land.

He also always talked about his friend who has a piece of land twenty times the size of his own but planted no food and raised no animals. Every time he talks about that, his expression changes to sadness. He cannot

34

understand how can a man could have so much land and not have much to eat.

Most people in my father's area and across the island are building bigger houses, so more land is required. I told my father that when I rebuild his house, I will not use an extra inch of his land, so he smiled. I know he loves to plant his own foods and share or sell to whoever asked him. I like the way my father lives. He is very self-sufficient.

God is good to me, so I am good to God by praying to him every day. I am enjoying the time that I have while I still have it, because the old folks say, "Tomorrow is not promised to anyone." St. Lucia is a place where I am not stressed out; it is a place where I can be myself.

I walk down the street with no shoes on my feet, my hair all nappy and uncombed, with no shirt on my back. I just realize that no one is crossing the street because I am coming. No one is holding a pocketbook closer to his or her body. And (my favorite one) no one is looking at me suspiciously. Some are wondering if I am crazy. No, I am not bugging, I am just relaxing myself.

A day on the island to me is like a day without time. I stopped wearing my watch on the island because I do not care what day it is. All I know is that today I do not have to worry about time. So what can I say? Today is just another day that I am enjoying.

The roosters all over the island wake up the whole island. From four thirty to six thirty you can hear them crowing and crowing and crowing until the sun comes up. The sun comes up the same way it went down last night: happy.

My father's roosters sleep over his house in a tree right next to my window. One morning I decided to watch the roosters get of the tree, and the first thing a rooster does the moment he touches ground is give it to the hens as much as he can. I noticed two roosters in my father's yard. One had all the chicks and the other was trying to steal a quickie as best he could. But every time he tried the other one would attack him.

The one with all the chicks led the way and dug the ground to find food for them, and when he found food he called to his chicks and they came running. Men are always working hard to impress the chicks. I have time to notice all that because I am enjoying time itself. Time waits for no one, so enjoy the time you have on earth and try to help someone in your lifetime. I choose to praise God.

I have memories of St. Lucia wherever I go. It keeps me motivated and hopeful. St. Lucia! St. Lucia, love of my life! I would love to marry you, but I already have a wife. I like the way you treat me when I am feeling blue. I am going to walk to your rivers and sing a song to you. Love is on my mind, love all the time. Even if I am down, love always comes around. I cannot chase her away, because I really want love to stay. Stay with me and comfort me. Love I am after. Can't you see how wonderful you are? You never lie to me. That's why I love you. Love, set me free.

Very few people know about the island St. Lucia, so let me tell you about her. The island is about 238,000 square miles and has a population of about 150,000 people. Most people who have been to the island always ask me what I am doing in America or why I would leave such a beautiful island like that. It is simple: the money. Just like any other foreigner from any other country, from around the world.

St. Lucia made its big appearance in the late '70s in a movie called *Fire Power*, staring the infamous O.J. Simpson. And two more movies were made after that. I think they were *Doctor Doolittle* and *Superman.*

There is a garden or a private park in Castries that is named after our very own Nobel Prize winner of literature in 1992 and his name is Derek Walcott.

In his park there is a tree that is about hundred years old, and in Creole it is called the massaz'e tree, and in English I don't know what it means. No one on the island knows its name and no one has ever figured it out. Yet it's the kind of tree that became part of the island culture. His place is also a place you would like to take your wedding pictures, with all the different-colored flowers in your background.

On the island of St. Lucia, where there are no private beaches, I could go wherever I wanted, and I did. I remember growing up as a child and walking along the many hotel beaches so I could watch the white women sunbathing. One thing they always do is expose their breasts to the sun. Some of the older guys, especially some Rastas, are always trying to get one of those white women. Now I am back on the island enjoying my vacation, and it is still the same. White women are sunbathing and the guys are still trying to experience their first white meat.

There are a lot of people who get married on our many lovely yellow-sand beaches. You know I love to talk about calm blue water. Some days I could walk out into the water until the water reached my chest, and when I looked down I could still see the corn on my little toe. The beauty of an island is in the beauty of its water, so if you want to know what it looks like, just look up into the sky on a clear, bright, sunny day. That's St. Lucia's water.

Those couples look extra, extra happy getting married on a tropical island like this. It is nice to see those couples getting married, but being married like this, on a lovely Caribbean island, just the way I see it in those romantic movies. Now the bride can show her pictures and boast to he friends about her beautiful wedding on the island of St. Lucia, a.k.a. the Helen of the West.

I do not know the whole story, but this is what I do know. Helen was a very beautiful queen. She may be from France or England; I do not know. Out of all the islands in the West Indies, St. Lucia is named after a queen, Helen of the West.

Chapter Five
Friday-Night Dinner

Friday nights are my favorite nights on the island. Friday is the night I go out for dinner. There are two places you can go on a Friday night, so my friends are taking me to a place up north. The place is called Croislet, where a few streets are closed off and it becomes a big street party. We walk around for a while so I can check out the place. People are selling foods along side the streets and the bars are open for a long period of time so you can drink as much as you want and eat as much barbeque as you can.

We walk to the end of this street. The crowd was standing next to the big speaker box. We found a short wall and sat down on it. "Does anybody wants a beer?" I ask , everyone said yes.

I was chilling like a villain and sipping on my Heineken. We decide to hang out on this wall for a while so we can investigate the crowd, or mind people's business. We can tell people are enjoying our Friday-night jam from the way they are mingling with the people with a beer in one hand and dancing totally offbeat to our calypso and French music. No one is laughing at them as they dance the night away; plus they are not in their own country, so they can be crazy for one night.

Fantasy island for most foreigners. I notice the friendliness between the whites and blacks dancing around the speaker box, and tonight Sharon White will be getting her groove on. One of the reasons Sharon came to our island, besides her great suntan, was to experience an island mon. So tonight she will be getting it right on the beach, under the moonlight; her perfect fantasy island, she use to fantasize about big Bobber Mandingo black, in her society but never had one so now she is on the island dancing with Bobber and Sharon is stone.

It is also the same for John White. He would love to taste a piece of that dark chocolate sister shaking herself so seductively in her green coconut skirt. Now they both could leave our island with pure satisfaction and no one would have to know about it except their closest friends.

There are policemen patrolling the streets, so our foreign friends can enjoy a night of eating and drinking in the streets. I am getting hungry watching people eat, so it's time for me to eat. So we walk around to find the right food to eat because most of the guys are Rastas and they do not eat meat.

It is not hard to be a vegetarian on the island. In fact it is much easier to become one, because all the fruit trees have their season, so when the mango season is done, other fruit trees take their turn. All year around there are fruits and vegetables available all over the country. One more thing I must mention... never mind. Oh, I will tell you on the *Oprah Winfrey Show*. She said she couldn't find a book that could motivates her. Well, Miss Winfrey, this one will make you scratch your head.

So they took me to the back and we brought some fried fish and a vegetarian dish from their homeboy, Jah Love, who owns a small vegetarian shack right next to the beach. Sitting by the sea and eating fish from the sea reminds me of Jesus sharing his love and fish, so I too share my love and fish, and they too share their love by passing me a special island joint, the big one.

Now that my mood has changed, listening to the waves sing a song. *Crash, crash, here I come. No one can stop me; I am to strong.* The waves are sweet music to my ears; they make me forget about my problems. I didn't have to think about all the bills I must pay; nor did I think about having to go to work again tomorrow for that lousy boss.

There is nothing in this world more relaxing than the songs of the ocean waves breaking one after the other. The only thing that was missing that night was the sound of the African drums playing in the background and the chanting of a Rastamon's spiritual song.

We walk back to the crowd and stay a little while longer and then leave. On our ride home the guys ask me if I enjoyed myself. They said if I didn't, next Friday they were going to take me to a place much better than that.

Today is Friday and tonight we are going down south to a place called Ans-La-Ray. It is famous for its seafood and I know that they have my favorite seafood. We take a transport going down south and I notice the driver is drinking and driving. In St. Lucia they drive on the right side of the street, not the left, so if you go to our island, don't freak out when your taxi is driving on the right-hand side of the street (I did).

There are two ways to get to the south. You can take the highway (the first real one on the island) or you can go through the mountain, which I find very dangerous. But that's the way he takes. We are driving through the mountain at night where there are no streetlights and our taxi driver is drinking. The road through the mountain is cut like a snake, so every minute we are turning a different corner.

The two-way street through the mountain is no bigger than a one-lane highway. Every time I see a car approaching us, I get a little nervous. *How can two cars fit on such a small road like this?* I wonder. Plus, there is nothing on the sides of the road but bottomless pits, or our death. But in the daytime on this mountain, it is such a beautiful view of the island above sea level.

When we got there the place is also designed the same. A couple of streets are closed off for the Friday-night festival. We walk through a couple of streets to get to Main Street. The first things my eyes see are big lobsters hanging out of big pots—I mean extra big lobsters hanging out of extra big pots.

I am surprised to see the size of those lobsters, and to me they are not that expensive. From the look on my face, the guys can tell that I am feeling this place. I walk around so I can check out everyone's grills and pots to see what I will eat first. But I am really looking for a certain kind of sea snail. It is boiled like lobster and crabs, so it comes right out of it shell. Uh, uh, uh, it's a pleasure to eat.

I found a woman who had some, so I placed my order. She told me that I was lucky because she only had five left. I took them all and sat at her table that she set up for her customers. I pulled it out from its shell and ate it from its tail to its head. Nothing was wasted but the shells.

Tonight I am going to eat everything I can. I mean tonight I am going to be greedy. This is the first time I am going to talk about food so much. Let me stop lying to myself. I love seafood and also my wife. One of our favorite restaurants is Red Lobster. We go to that place whenever we can, and I even know a song that they sing to you on your birthday.

Red Lobster is fun and true. Red Lobster is fun and true, especially when we sing for you. The good news is we sing off-key; the bad news is the cakes aren't free. So sound off; one, two. Sound off; three, four. Sound off; one, two, three, four, five, six. Something like that, just to show you that I am in the right place tonight.

There is also a certain kind of fish that I am looking for. I am going to try to enjoy myself like a child. I want to eat the things I used to enjoy as a child, so tonight, after such a long, long time away from my home, I am going to treat myself like I am a spoiled brat.

This kind of fish is not cooked, steamed, or fried, but is stuffed with Stove Top stuffing or breadcrumbs and roasted until the hard skin starts falling off. I see a few people roasting fish for sale, and when I was young I couldn't afford it. But tonight I hope my belly has enough room for the things I love to eat.

I bought two—one big one and one small—and sat down to enjoy myself. I split them open and started eating them from the inside with my fork. One thing about a good taste Your mouth never forgets a good taste. I almost forgot about the friends who had brought me here. "Listen mon," I said, "here is some money for you guys to do your own thing. And as for me, seafood is on my mind."

I went to see what else I could find here that I had a craving for. Fried fish? Not tonight. Steamed fish with island seasoning? Maybe later. Roasted corn? Not in the mood. Maybe one of those big giant lobsters? Mm, that sounds good. I do not want to eat a lot of food quickly, just in case I see some other seafood that I have missed so much.

"Excuse me, miss, what do you have in this pot?" I asked a woman.

"LAA-bee," she replied. It was something I had the craved also. It was another shellfish, and I don't know the correct name for it, but we call it LAA-bee.

"Try it," she said, "it's good for your peter. It makes you go all night long."

43

She must have told this story to the foreigner sitting at her table enjoying it so curiously. I always admired that in white folks. They would try anything and some try the stuffed fish that I talked about.

So I asked her, "Can I get a plateful?"

She served me a medium-sized plastic bowl, soup style. I sat down to clean out my bowl and in the background, in the middle of the street, some big speaker boxes were playing some good old-time reggae , my favorite music, to entertain the crowd.

Oh mon, I thought. *This is good.* I am on an island away from my bills and headaches. I am getting a brand new feeling that I have never felt before—a feeling that I would love to always enjoy. I never knew this feeling existed before, but tonight I have it and I am not letting this go. peace of mind. St. Lucia is the island that takes away my pain and shows me how to enjoy myself by myself. You know what else comes to mind? When the mind is free the whole body gets loose.

I talk about St. Lucia to so many different people. They all would like to go. And you know what else? Some are going and some are fascinated by the way I describe it. There is food ,food . all around me—seafood. You know where to find me.

Most people go to our beautiful island and never enjoy the island itself. Some advice for my foreign people is don't get confined to only your hotel; go out and meet the people with a different culture than yours and enjoy some of our many different foods.

LAA-bee. Should I have one more bowl, I ask myself. *Why not?. It is your night.* After my second bowl, my people come back to meet me. They ask me if I'm okay. I say "of course" with my new island accent. We walk around to check out the fine women the island have to offer. Their are a lot of mixed couples walking around holding hands, and no one is giving them that evil eye. That's another thing I like about the island: They accept you and treat foreigner very well. I did not give them a second thought, because I knew everyone loves that chocolate.

Someone passed me a piton, St. Lucia's own beer, and a piece of steamed fish in aluminum foil, island style. We walked down to the beach to an old broken-down jetty and sat down to enjoy the island the Rastamon way.

After the fish came the smoke. After the smoke come the meditation, and after the meditation came the chanting of one of Bob Marley's songs. *"Old pirates, yes they rod I, sold I to the merchants ships."* After that brotherly love episode, we walked back to the place of action, right next to the speaker box.

The women have the spotlight because of the way they walk back and forth so the guys can see who is the hottest one in the place tonight. The hot girl believes that no girl in the place should look better than her. So she makes sure that she has on the most outstanding outfit in the place tonight. And you know men will be calling her all night long, so that makes her feel like she is the one all men are after, or the hottest girl in the place.

Now I can go and buy one of those big lobsters that I have been thinking about all night, I said to myself. It didn't take me long to find that big lobster that I craved so much, because big lobsters are the main attraction every Friday night. I ordered the greedy size, the one that was too much for me. She gave me the lobster, a fork, and some lemon but no butter. I sat down at the table and squeezed the lemon all over that big, sweet, juicy lobster. I put down my fork and at it caveman style, hands and teeth. I didn't finish the whole thing, but I sure try hard as hell. I stay at that table a little while longer and watch some of my lobster tail go to waste.

The guys call me, so we walk down that same busy street to a reggae club not too far from the corner. We walk in and I walk straight to the speaker box, the place of all the action.

I like to watch people dance so I can learn the newest dance steps. Most of the dance steps I already know because I am from New York, the street dance capital of the world. I spend the rest of the night in that club, rubber-dubbing to the music I love so much. Like brother Bob says, one good thing about music when it hits you, you feel no pain. So hit me with music. And the music hit me all night long. You could call me Rodney King on his payday: happy.

We leave the place about three in the morning and I stop to buy two more of those stuffed fish that I like so much. If I had room I would eat this right now, but I will save it for my breakfast in the morning. I got home and for a couple of days I thought about and say to myself, *I would love to retire on an island like this. But I am going need a business to support me for the rest of my life.*

St. Lucia, St. Lucia. It so nice I have to say it twice. Every January first, second and sometimes third, the island celebrates an annual festival called Square. It's like Coney Island. When I was young I couldn't wait to go to Square to play some games, eat some foods, and show off my new clothes and shoes that someone would give me for my Christmas.

I think my father used to give me five dollars a day so I could enjoy myself, and back then five dollars still wasn't worth much, but he gave me what he had. Some years we couldn't afford to go.

The first thing I would buy with my money was a piece of fry chicken. It may be a stereotype, but this black man loves his fried chicken. The next thing I would spend my money on was a big red apple for a dollar. Back then we only got apples once a year at Christmas. So the people would sell them for whatever price they wished, and I had to buy one. It was an apple and it was from America, and I was tired of eating mangoes and bananas all year round. So that made the apple the king of the fruits. Snow White got poisoned by one; Adam got tricked with one. And so all men have to wear their Adam's apple as a reminder of Adam's sin.

Now that I am in St. Lucia and a few people would like to take me to Square, and this time I have a lot more than five dollars. My mother told me Square was created so parents would have a place to take their children. The kids in my area would like to go, but things are tight with their parents. So I have decided to play black Santa Claus. I told the parents, "Let's make a deal. I am willing to take you and your kids to Square, but I am only paying and buying for the kid, and you ladies have to take care of your own selves." They all agreed.

We walked around for a while and then I realized that four of the parents did not speak to each other. I couldn't take all that madness—four women with kids that did not get along—so I gave all the parents some money and told them "go your own way and later on tonight we will all meet each other by the bus stop."

I left and walked around exploring the place, still remembering from when I was a child. I am so grateful to be back on my island and I am enjoying it like a careless child. Oh man, I remember this game. You put your twenty-five cents or dollar on a number from one to six. The man rolls the dice and if your number comes up you win double your money. It's a kid's game, but you know me by now. I had to play a couple of games just for the fun of it.

47

I saw this other game I used to play as a child. A bucket was filled with water with a flat plate floating on top. You stand behind a line marked on the ground and pitch your quarter on to the plate. If it stays on you win, and if it falls into the water, you know. I never won as a child, and still cannot win as adult, but at least I know why now.

Square was just the way I remember it: plenty of kids and plenty of adults all dressed up in the latest American fashion, and also many shacks that line the place selling many different kinds of foods and drinks. Fried chicken and apples are everywhere. They are my childhood favorite. But now I wish I could eat mangoes and sweet island bananas all year around. It's a lot better for my health.

I walk around some more to see if anything has changed from when I was a child. Some company from England came down with different rides for kids and some for the grownups as well. They also put on a spectacular show of fireworks and introduced bumper cars to the island, and you know I was knocking the island kids around.

Later on I found all the kids' parents standing next to the ride, far apart from each other. But at least the kids were enjoying the place, and that made me happy. Then the rain started coming down from nowhere. We made it to our transport and headed to our homes. During our ride home, someone on the bus said, "It always rains every year of the festival." And someone explained that this was the rainy season.

I got home that night and listened to the raindrops falling on my father's galvanized roof. The only time I felt a little sad and lonely on the island was when I am listening to the romantic rain drops falling and no one was there to keep me warm (I mean my wife).

Chapter Six
Island Workout

Tomorrow is Sunday and this is my last week on the island of sweet St. Lucia, the place that shows me how to appreciate my one life. So I am going to do the same thing that I do every Sunday: spend my whole day on the beach, running, communicating, and doing some of my own water workouts.

I always run into this one guy on the beach. He is always looking for something,—I mean anything he can find to make some money. And whenever he sees me coming his face always lights up like a Christmas tree because he knows I will give him something. And most of the time I do not mind, but don't make it a bad habit.

"Jah-com, how come you are always on the beach?" I ask him, and he replies, "It's peaceful and you never know what you will find." He told me that the sea is the riches place on earth, so I thought about it and decided it is true. There are so many sunken treasure ships, and so many people lost their wedding rings to the sea, like me.

He also told me that the best time to search the beach is after a storm. That's when the sea cleans its bottom out and brings new sands to the shore. And with that new sand comes new gifts, maybe my ring.

I always bring six dollars to the beach every Sunday, just in case I run into him, and I always do. I do spend four dollars on myself, two for fried fish, one for an island Juice, and the fourth is for two fried dumplings. My last two dollars are divided. I share one with him and the other one is for anyone who is hungry and asks me for something to eat.

I am sitting down on a big piece of tree trunk and watching the old Rastas and young ones play their favorite game of soccer. They are always arguing about "if they ran the country ,they would legalize weed as a medicine for peace talks between the two countries," like the Indian peace pipe.

I would run down the beach in one direction until I came to the end and then turn around and run back to the spot where I sat. Now I was going to spend the four dollars on myself. seemed I am burned out and thirsty.

After I had eaten and drank my Sunday special, it was time to roll up my Sunday joy right on the beach. I do not have to worry about the police bothering me, and if they do bother me, I will just say to them in my foreign accent that I did not know it was illegal in this country.

This is the time that Jan-com tells me things, when he is passing my joint back to me. "You see that flagpole way out there?" he said. "None of those guys on the beach that say they are brave—not one of them would go out there with me. They are all afraid of sharks and cramps" So he asks me if I would like to try it. "No! That's too far for me," I answered him. He kept on bugging me and kept on talking about going out to that pole.

You could actually stand out there, he told me. It's a big coral reef. He looked at me and said, "You could do it." I looked him and thought *not me*. I had spent all those years away from real ocean water; plus I had never swum that far before. But you know what? I will try anything once. That's one of the keys to success: try and try again.

I decided to take that chance, believing I could do it. But I had never swum that far out before. It looked about half a mile, so I jumped into the water right after him and started to swim toward the flagpole. I remembered what a guy told me on the seashore. He told me the sea has no branches. I kept on swimming with my eyes on Jah-com. He kept on swimming and looking back for me.

My arms are getting tired and the flagpole seems to be getting farther and farther away instead of closer and closer. Swimming is part of my workout every time I come to the beach, but on Sundays I do more swimming and more running. That is why Sundays are my best days on the beach. My whole body is in pain. That is why swimming is my best exercise.

You have to use every part of your body, from your toes to your head. Every muscle must work. Sometimes I get into the water about waist high and run against the water to work on my legs. The faster you run, the more strength you use in your legs. I also would do my own butterfly by going out a little farther into the water (about neck high) and extending my hands like Jesus on his cross and then making them clap in front of me. The faster I go, the harder it's getting. I am not trying to get big; I am just trying to stay strong. I would swim a lot farther out, where I know my feet cannot touch the bottom. Then I would extend my hands like a bird extends its wings and begin to fly, my hands going up and down at my sides and at the same time my feet paddling my invisible bike.

When I stop, I could quickly sink to the bottom, so I would do this special workout for about ten to twenty minutes and then swim back to the shore of our beautiful yellow-sand beach, where I would lie down to get a blacker, darker tan.

We are almost at the flagpole, where I know I could get a little rest, standing on the coral reef. Oh boy, I am in the middle of that blue ocean water, where I can see the people on shore as small as snails. Jah-com forgot to mention that the waves are breaking right over the coral reef, and they come in different sizes.

Sometimes to get away from a wave you have to go under the wave, and that is exactly what I did. But sometimes the waves came in two or threes, and so when I came up from the first one, the number two would hit me in the face. So I ended up with a nose full of water. And if you could see me, you would know I have a big nose.

I try to ride one of those big waves by lying on my chest the way I used to as a young boy. It's like a surfer riding his board on his belly. I did not have much success catching a wave back to shore, but I was successful in touching the bottom in deep waters.

On our way back, Jah-com told me that he could touch bottom anywhere in this ocean. After we have been swimming for a while, he wanted to know if I wanted to try it. "Why not?" I said. He went down and came up with a handful of sand. I went down but halfway down my ears started ringing, so I rushed back to the surface out of breath.

He looked at me and I looked at him with no sand in my hand. "Wait a minute, mon. I am trying to catch my breath," I told him. I went back down with my hands extended like Superman and my eyes closed. I keep on diving and diving down until my fingers touched the sand. I grabbed a handful of sand and rushed back to the surface. I opened my hand and threw the sand at him, suggesting that I could touch bottom wherever he touch it. He kept on touching the bottom in different places, so wherever he touch it I touched it also. Finally we made it to the shore, where I laid down to catch my breath.

St. Lucia: what a beautiful country, where I could lay on the beach and watch the people entertain me. On Sundays everyone comes to the beach to relax. Some of the women are showing off their figures and some are jogging up and down the beach. The men are playing soccer and some are playing cricket. These are the two favorite sports on the island'. I would lay down on the sand and enjoy the game I want I would watch the soccer game for a while and when I got bored with that, I would just roll over and turn my attention to the cricket game. And if that didn't hold my attention, I would turn my eyes to the many white people enjoying our blue seas and yellow-sand beaches.

Some of them are skiing, some are windsurfing and falling most of the time, while others are reading their books and it is not written by me. It would be nice for you to read my book while lying on your beach chair on the island of St. Lucia. How would this effect you? I do not know.

Here he comes, the mon Jah-com, with a thousand stories to tell and a few strands of dreads that are left on his head. "Yeah, mon!" I said. "You could cut those strings off it look like somebody tortured you by pulling your dreads out one at a time." He didn't find that funny, but I do not care.

The worst thing you can tell a Rastamon is to cut his hair. His dreads are a symbol of his rebellious ways against society's teachings. I always wanted to ask him what happened to his body. It looked like he been through hell and back. He didn't want to tell me, but I bugged him in so many different ways that he decided to talk.

I already knew his story, but I wanted to hear it from him instead. This is what I knew before he told me his story: Do unto others as you would like them to do unto you. The good you do will follow you. But he has been a bad boy since he was young, so he wears his punishment for the rest of his natural life.

He told me plain and simple, "I got chopped up by some young kid," but the people had told me the whole story about that. Jah-com was a bad boy, a troublesome kid, a menace to society, a bully on the island.

The people told me that back then this guy would slap your girlfriend if he didn't like the way she dressed. He was that type of guy that if you stepped on his shoes, you were asking for your death. When you see him coming you automatically cross over to the other side. If he were killed, the whole community would be happy instead of sad.

One day his time was up, so it was time to pay the piper. I was told that he was messing with a young man or bullying a young kid. Like in the story of David and Goliath, he thought he could never be defeated. So the young man couldn't take it anymore and ran home and got St. Lucia's favorite weapon, the machete, or like we call it, the cutlass. It looked like the guy cut him up without any mercy. His right hand was almost paralyzed from trying to block that machete. Now he is cool and a lot friendlier to the people he meets on the street. He is one of the few lucky bad boys that made it to old age. God has been merciful to him and gave him a second chance in life, but he has to wear his punishment as a reminder of his bad-boy days.

So much to do, so little time. Where do the time go when you are having fun? I am leaving sweet St. Lucia, and that makes me sad, but at the same time I am very anxious to come back to America. It's about four o'clock and I am ready to leave after a long day on the beach.

My father always has a plate of food waiting on me when I get home, and this dinner is no different from the last one: foods from the ground and fish from the sea. I am complaining about the food, but sometimes I would like to come home to some American food, so that's why I cannot wait to come back to America and eat some food with plenty of calories. I have lost a lot of weight and regained my original accent, mon. I love you long time, St. Lucia.

Chapter Seven
Confidence the Key to Success

After my dinner and a little rest, it's time for the big soccer games that takes place not too far from my father's house. Soccer is the world's number-one sport, and on Sundays you find the best match-up games. I am not a big soccer fan but I am learning to like it.

I remembered practicing on this very same field, trying to make the school soccer team. Every morning my mother would wake me up about five thirty so I could practice for my school soccer team. There were some guys who only practiced some mornings and made the team. And I woke up early every morning and worked hard and did everything the coach said to do and still didn't make the team. You know something? I never understood that for a long time. In fact, that hurt me so much that I never learned to play the game of soccer.

Today one of the teams has some guys on it whom I have known since I was small. This is really amusing to me. After such a long time people still remember me, but I can't remember some of them and that is very embarrassing.

One guy talked to me for about twenty minutes and I still couldn't remember him and at the same time I was too embarrassed to ask him his name.

"You remember me. I was in your class," he said to me. "We used to cut class and hide by the river until it was time to go home."

"Oh yeah. I remember," I answered him, but I really couldn't remember.

There was live entertainment on my Sunday afternoon. What a perfect vacation. Someone shouted to me in the crowd, "Oh, it's my homeboy the Rastamon. Come sit with us." He said this with smoke coming out from his nose.

I could sit on any side of the field I wished. On one side you would find the businessmen and the working-class people who don't smoke in public—who have to keep a clean image. On the other side you would find the Rastas, the weed sellers, the hustlers, and me. I was an outcast when I was young, and I will be an outcast until the day I get to heaven.

Some days I would sit down on the sophisticated side so I could listen to the people's conversation and their ideas about politics. And it was not the same conversation as the outcast, but my mind was open enough to understand both sides.

Sitting under a shady tree not too far from the school I use to go to as a child. I remember the principal who used to run the school. If you did something wrong or bad, your teacher would send you to the principal's office, where he had the right to punish you whatever way he liked.

Hanging on his wall in his office was a big fat leather belt that he would use to punish you by giving you four lashes on your hands, two on the left and two on the right. The one thing about going to the principal's office I remember is the way he looked at you when you first walked in.

I can envision him right now behind his desk with his head in some book and his glasses hanging on the tip of his nose. And as soon as you walked in, he picked up his head just a little bit to see who you were, and sometimes it was me.

All he did for that moment was point at you and point to the corner where you would have to go and kneel down until he was ready for you.

Kneeling in his office and waiting to get my ass beaten was enough punishment for my mind to bear. I never finished school, so I never did learn to read or write. I never passed any test to go to a higher grade higher than standard four..

I was told that I was dyslexic and couldn't learn a thing in school, so I dropped out at the age of thirteen. I always, always, had a gut feeling about writing a book. But how? Then I took my first vacation. St. Lucia opened my eyes, ears, and my understanding, and the one thing I am most thankful to God for is my confidence.

The biggest word I could have spelled two days before I started writing this book was the word *together*, and the longest letter I ever wrote was a half-page letter begging my uncle in England for a radio. I never received that radio and I never knew if the letter ever made it to England. Most likely I spelled the address wrong.

When I came back from my vacation and thought about the things I did in St. Lucia—things I never did before—thoughts I had never had before came to me. So I sat at my table and took a pen and a notebook and began writing this story. And I started to learn about myself to see if I was what people say I am: the black sheep. But I am not a black sheep; I am just a lost sheep who has found the Good Shepherd.

It's the hardest thing to do but the most rewarding thing you can do for yourself. The first thing I discovered was that I did not have any confidence in me, so I started a long and difficult journey to find it in me.

Is there any confidence in me? I started asking myself, I couldn't believe it. There was no confidence in me. I still couldn't believe that, so I went back a second time to look for my confidence. I have seen people show their confidence by the way that they stand up for their beliefs. And

I have heard people say that if you believe in yourself you can do anything you want.

I never, never, in my wildest dreams believed them. *They must be talking to someone else, not me,* I thought. I always thought that the people on TV who say "if you just believe in yourself your dreams can come true" were people who were born with a silver spoon in their mouths. I never believed that my dreams could come true, because I am always saying negative things to myself like "my nose is too big" or "I can never make it, because I am from a small island and have an accent, and the kids used to make fun of me whenever I spoke." They would say, "Go back to your banana boat, you coconut. You people came here to take our jobs." That didn't help my confidence.

I ran into a whole lot of trouble and problems with myself. As a child the kids used to tease me about my nose, saying things like, "Look at his nose. That's not a nose. That's a two-car garage." Or they would say, "His nose is so big that every time he sneezes he gets a headache," whispering it to their friends but loudly enough for me to hear it.

I was so embarrassed about the way I look for such a long time. "That's an ugly little boy," I once heard someone say. I remember one woman in particular. She gave me a hard time when I was growing up. This evil woman in her thirties used to live on top of the same hill as my father. My father has a friend whom I talked about before. He lived farther up that hill from that wicked woman's house.

Sometimes my father would send me to his friend's house for something, and there was only one road on that hill. It passed right in front of that wicked woman's house.

I was about seven years old, and every time that lady saw me coming she would start laughing and laughing and pointing at me, saying, "Here comes the son of King Kong." She would point at my big nose, making me feel less than a human being.

She would laugh so loudly that her whole family would join in and laugh at that seven-year-old boy, calling me an ugly, dirty little boy who looked like King Kong's son. She used to tease me so much that I would start crying and crying because I was a big-nosed kid with a lot of pimples.

I always wished I could hit that evil woman right in the middle of her big head with a stone. People can be so cruel to children that you have to be careful of what you say to your child. The things you teach children will sharpen their minds. If you teach them the right way in life, most likely they will be good parents to their children. But when you teach them the wrong things about life, most likely they will raise bad children.

So this is what I found when I was looking for my confidence . that big-nosed little boy with a face full of pimples. That lady always made me feel ashamed of myself, so I started walking with my head down, looking for my lost confidence.

If you see a person walking with his or her head always down, that person has no confidence in him- or herself, and if you know someone who can look you in your eyes and correct you when you are wrong without flattering you, that person has a lot of confidence in him- or herself. Now, if you hear someone always talking about themselves and what they have, that's not confidence. That's conceitedness.

Confidence, confidence. Where are you? I need you so I can succeed in life. I am still looking for my confidence because I know I have some in me somewhere. But where? I have looked for it more then once and couldn't find it. *Oh boy, I finally see something shining way down inside of me. This has to be my confidence*, I said to myself.

But there is so much garbage in front of my little light. Oh well, let me start moving some of those things out of the way so I can get a better view. I moved a couple of pieces of garbage and decided to throw them out of me. *I remember this piece of junk*, I said to myself.

I was about fourteen years old and all of my friends were into partying and talking to girls now, so they invited me to some of the parties that they were going to. You know what? I am apologize, but I do not like this piece. Instead let me tell you about the girl who kissed me and made me cry.

She was fourteen years old and had ashy and pimpled skin. My friends were into girls and nice clothes. Most of the time when we went to parties they would end up dancing with a couple of girls in the place. It seemed like every time I asked girls to dance they always turned me down. After so many letdowns I started to feel a little ugly about myself.

Could it be my clothes, or could it be my big stupid nose that always gets in my way? Or am I just that ugly kid with a face full of pimples? I would wonder I always used to say to myself as a young man, *If I ever make it to America, I will use my money to make my nose smaller.* But now I love it. I accepted it and I am going to die with it. We know someone who wishes he could have back big black African nose.

On the way home after the party the guys would talk about how many girls that they danced with at the party. And then they asked me, "How many did you dance with tonight, Papa Crow?" That's the name they used to call me.

I always fantasized about being a reggae singer, like the late great Bob Marley, and my stage name would be Papa Crow or The black Crow. So they asked me again, "How many girls did you dance with, Crow?" *Should I lie to them or should I tell them the truth? If I tell them the truth, they will tease me and make fun of me.* I didn't want that to happen. I wanted to be accepted and be cool with my friends. So of course I lied.

Listen to what happened. I told my friends I danced with two girls at the party. One I danced about two songs and with the other one I danced in the corner not too far from the speaker box. She was feeling on me and I was feeling on her all night. I had my lips on her neck and she had her lips next to my ear. And then that slow reggae song came on by Gregory Isaacs: 'Night Nurse.' Yeah, mon! She was holding on me so tight and I was grinding on her, just right. Yeah, mon! She even let me grab that A.A.A." They all got really excited and started laughing loudly and patting me on the back, saying, "You the mon, you the mon." What a lie, but I accepted it and am not embarrassed.

I didn't want them to know that I had no game and I had never danced with a girl yet. In fact, I was scared of girls and didn't know what to say to them. And they never said, "Hi, boy, you look nice," which would have helped me in my confidence department.

The closest I ever got to a girl at fourteen was through this game called "I dare you." One guy dares this pretty girl to kiss me, but first they had to hold me down because I started running away from her. And then they finally caught me and held me down for that kiss. I started crying. My friends never let me forget that kiss, and I never forgot my first kiss—the one that made me cry.

Now this is some of the garbage I found when I was looking for my confidence: the guy who is too shy to talk to girls, the guy who cannot afford nice clothes, and that big nose kid with a face full of pimples.

I was starting not to like myself, because of the way I looked. I wished I was a little lighter with a smaller nose and a lot nicer hair, instead of this hard hair. I put a clothespin on my nose many nights so I could have a much smaller nose. But it kept on growing and growing like Pinocchio's nose—not straight and long, but sideways and wide.

Nevertheless, all the pain, shame, and resentment that I have found inside of me, which I have stored up for so many years, will not stop me from finding my confidence. No pain, no gain. So I have to push my way through, no matter the cost.

Now that I know my shame, which is me, I have to find my confidence, which is me. I could see a little clearer when I moved some of those pieces of garbage out of me.. But there was a lot more garbage to be thrown out.

I brought me some gloves and a whole lot of garbage bags to remove all this junk that I had found in me. The guy who stuttered and was too afraid to talk to girls was another thing that took away my confidence. "Where did this girl come from?" I asked my friends. "From the country," they said. *Yea mon, I like that girl.*

Every time I saw her my heart beat faster and faster. *One day I will talk to her*, I always said to myself. *Oh boy, here she comes, and today I am going to do it.* "Hi, Hi, Hi, Hiiii, gggg girl. Www what's yyy your nnname?" I said pouring in sweet. I cannot remember if she answered me or not, because I took so long to ask her a couple of questions. I never got that girl. Some light-skined brother with a job roped her in.

I am fifteen years young and have never gone out with a girl. Every time I try and talk to one I get all nervous and start stuttering. I am getting into a lot of trouble those days, so my parents don't know exactly what to do with me. Eventually my mother told me that she had to get me off of the island before someone killed me, or my father will hurt me really badly.

We are blessed. My mother got us a visa to come to America, where the streets are paved with gold and the food is very cheap. Out of her eleven children, she brought her most troublesome one up first. Before I left the island, a friend of mine gave me some advice about America: "Make sure your doors are locked, and whatever you do, don't try drugs."

I will not stop digging and shoveling all of this garbage from out of inside of me, so let me dig some more. *What is this big black garbage bag doing in that corner all alone?* I said to myself. I picked up my shovel and was about to bust the bag wide open, but then I thought to myself, *This may be my confidence tied up in that black plastic bag. But why would my confidence be hiding in a plastic bag? Maybe it is scared,* I answered myself. *Scared-fidence.* No. *Confidence,* you know—the one that makes you believe in yourself, the one that makes you succeed in life. So I untied the bag and this is what I found: the boy who tried to be accepted in the hood with his West Indian accent.

I am so impressed with the American accent and the way they dress in school with their pants hanging down their butts. You know my story. I wanted to fit in, so I had to do something to fit in.

I notice in the locker room after gym class. Most of the guys smoke cigarettes and that looks cool to me. And also the guys are slapping one another high-fives and calling each other "homeboy." I wanted to be part of the American life so much because of the way they were portrayed in movies. And now that I am here, fresh off the banana boat, I am going to be one of those cool kids that I used to see on TV.

I started to buy a pack of cigarettes every day and was the first one in the locker room after gym. As soon as the guys started coming in I opened my pack of cigarettes so they all could see me. They all would say to me, "Yo, homeboy, could I get one of your cigarettes?" And of course I gave them to them, and that made me feel a little accepted in my gym class.

Less then a year in America, and I am smoking cigarettes, and on my block it is just the same. There is one girl on my block that I like a lot, but she doesn't like me. I heard her say to her friend, "that boy is ugly," and she also called me "coconut boy."

One day she was in my hallway with one of her friends, talking and smoking weed. She asked me, "Yo, homeboy, you want some?" I never gave it a second thought. I said "pass it." It had been a year and a couple of months in America, and I was smoking cigarettes and blunts in the school hallway, just like I used to see on TV.

Now that I am smoking with them, I would like to talk like them and get rid of my West Indian accent. I am embarrassed to talk around people, because they make fun of me whenever I talk. I spend many nights up trying to lose my accent by pronouncing the words with an American accent ("Mon,—no, man. Mon—no, man.") until I got it right. "Yo, man, what's up!" I did not say that much for about two years. When I was hanging with my new American friends I didn't say more than five words around them, because I was too ashamed of the way that I spoke.

Confidence, where are you? I need you so I can stand up proudly as a West Indian man and not a man of shame. I do not think I have any confidence in myself, so I am going to give up the search for it. I have been searching and searching for a long time now, and I cannot find anything that's good in me. All I can find is the kid who wants to be cool and is too ashamed to speak.

Then the night before I was about to give up my search, I heard a voice inside of me saying, *don't give up yet*. God gave everybody the same amount of confidence, so I said to my voice, *He must have forgotten me, because I cannot seem to find anything that can make me proud of myself.* And don't start telling me that you can do anything if you put your heart, mind, and time into it. I've heard that before and I don't even want to hear: "If you just believe in yourself, you can make your dreams come true." So I told my voice, *That's the problem. I cannot believe in something that's not good: myself.* The voice wanted to tell me some more, but I told it to leave me alone, because it did not know what it was talking about.

After I got over my resentment of that voice—the one that seemed to know everything, the one that told me what was right and what was wrong—one thing stuck in my head was the voice saying *don't give up*, so I started back on my journey to find that thing they call confidence.

The more I threw out my garbage, the more garbage I see. A small note fell out of the garbage bag that I was dragging out of me, and it read: *You are a follower, not a leader. That's why you will always be a loser.*

I was about to rip that note apart, but I changed my mind and decided to put it in my pocket so I could prove this note was wrong about me. I am getting very angry with people that are saying those things about me, and I am not a loser or a follower; I am just confused.

Two years in America and I haven't learned a thing in high school. I am too busy trying to be accepted by the so-called cool group. My uncle who worked construction told my mother, "the boy is not learning anything in high school," so I left boys and girls high and became a construction worker just like my favorite uncle, Jarome.

I am getting closer, and closer to something that I have a lot of feelings for. Could it be my lost confidence that's pulling me toward it? It's getting hotter and hotter in here. *This must be it*, I said to myself, so I started running toward that feeling that I only get when I am in love. I was running so fast to that feeling that I fell and bust my AAA, I probably broke all the bones in my body. I couldn't move for about four years. People tried to help me up but couldn't because I was trapped in myself, laying in my pity, and drowning in my sorrows.

My first name is Shedrac, but some of the people call me Shed Crack, or just plain Crackhead. I actually thought that feeling I was running toward was my confidence, but as you can see, it was the beginning of my nightmares. What little confidence that I was building up in me was destroyed in a glass pipe.

Three years in America and making money, and I am still trying to be accepted by the so-called cool group. One night in the hallway of my building I use to live in, a guy I knew was doing something in the corner, so I asked him, "What is that?" He didn't tell me but passed it. I never thought about it; I just tried it.

The note was right about me. I am a loser and a follower. I never thought to myself that this could be bad for me, or that this was a drug and I should just say no. I had to ask him what is that, and just like a follower, I tried it and fell in love. That's right; I fell in love.

The first time I tried crack I was addicted instantly to its feeling, and it felt like love to me. After we finished what he had left, I went upstairs and borrowed twenty dollars from my cousin.

I gave the guy the money so we could get some more. It didn't take him long to get back. We smoked what he brought back and then I went to my bed. The next day, which happened to be my payday, someone else dropped by my mother's apartment and wanted me to try something. It was weed and crack rolled up in rolling paper and was called a *rule*, or *ruler*.

We smoked a couple of them because the crack gave the weed that super high, but I was not satisfied with that. I wanted to smoke it like I had the night before, so I asked him about it and he went and bought me a glass pipe call the stem, and I didn't wanted to stop smoking it, but I had to go to work the next morning.

It was not painful in the beginning of my destruction because I was addicted to love. I felt good when I had it but unstable when I didn't. That means I would do anything to get it, including robbing someone to get it. Now crack is being sold everywhere and more and more people are getting hooked on it. Teachers, doctors, lawyers, and people in all different communities of America are being affected by it.

Crack is its name and destroying families is its aim. Some people say that it was created by man to destroy the black race but it backfired and did the same to the white race.

I am starting to lose my appetite for food and gain a desirer for crack and crack alone. I meet a couple of people on my block who smoke crack every day like me, so we develop a crackhead friendship. Birds of a feather flock together.

Now I am losing a lot of weight and people are noticing it too. That's the first sign of the addiction: loosing weight. "Yo man, are you on crack?" they ask me. "No man, crack is wack," I say, but they can see it all over my face. My cheek bones are showing and I am about five times smaller than my clothes. By denying it all the way—lying to them—but actually lying to myself.

My appetite for crack is growing tremendously but I am still denying I have a problem. Whenever someone asks me about it, I tell them that I can quit anytime I want, but I can't.

My mother knows that her son is a crackhead, so that makes her nervous around me, and I do not give her any wrong. A crackhead is no different then a poisonous snake. You never know when he is going to strike or squeeze the life out of you.

I would not spend my hard-earned money on food nor clothe, to keep my body warm and my belly full. Instead I spent my whole paycheck on the one thing that had control over me: crack. The first pull on the pipe made me feel like I could do anything, but the high only lasts for a couple of seconds. That's why I had to get high all night, and get high I did.

I cannot stop no matter how hard I try, and God Almighty knows that I am trying to stop. *Today I am not going to get high.* That is what I always say to myself every day, but as soon as I get some money in my hands, my whole attitude changes from light to darkness.

I do not know how it knows, but it knows. Sometimes when I get my paycheck, I say to myself, *I am going straight home today*, but as soon as I get off that train, my whole mindset changes from going home to going straight to the crack spot.

Crack is destroying people left and right all over the country. It is destroying my mother as well and she doesn't use drugs. Sons are killing their mothers and mothers are pimping their daughters for it. Fathers are destroying their families for that wonder-drug called crack.

My addiction is so strong that I have to have it every day, no matter what. I met a lady that lived across the street from me. She used to be a schoolteacher who owned two houses and did a lot of drugs. I became one of her get-high friends who used to go to the spot for her. In about two years we smoked both houses through the glass stem, and a couple of years later she died from AIDS.

Tomorrow is my payday and I am telling myself that I am not going to get high today; I am going to give my mother the money to hold for me so I will not get high. It is now eight o'clock in the morning and I am still telling myself the same thing, but as soon as I get my paycheck my stomach would flap up side down and my patience would disappear, and then anxiousness would take over my whole body.

I had to tell my boss some story so I could hurry home to get high and satisfy my addiction. I made up a lie, so he let me go. I ran to the train because I was so anxious to get high. I could not remember what story I gave him, because I became such a good liar that sometimes I believed it myself.

I learn how to cry when telling a sad story about my mother dieing or my father passing away. They must have died about six times apiece, that was the story I told to anyone I could get money out of.

What is taking the train so long? The craving for crack is killing me. If only I could just run to the spot, I would. But I am about ten miles away from the spot. *Oh here it comes. It's about time. Open door, open. Close door, close. How many more stops? Five more,* I said to myself. *What is wrong with that conductor? Can't he go any faster then that? Someone is sick on the train. Why does this always have to happen to me? Damn!*

I should get off that slow train and start running to Brooklyn, but it is still too far from home. My stomach is hurting me so badly that I have to use the bathroom. This happens every time I want to get high. My stomach doesn't need any food or drink. All I need is a good hit of the pipe and everything will be all right.

Finally my stop. Open door, open. I run to the spot. "Yo my man, give me two dimes." I run to my apartment. I am always running to get high, because the anxiety is taking over my whole body and soul.

After all my money is gone and I cannot get any money from anyone because it is three o'clock in the morning and I have to work. I am tossing and turning for the rest of the morning, trying to get some sleep. This is when the nightmares begin. Coming down from the high is worse than the anxiety to get high, and the anxiety to get high is worse than my addiction to it, which makes me a full-blown crack-head.

Why I just didn't give my mother the money like I said before? And then that addiction in me said "you couldn't," and I said *why not*, and it said to me, "You are my slave and I can make you do anything I want. Why do you think so many women are on the streets selling themselves so cheaply? It's not because they want to; it's because I made them do it. You remember your friend the schoolteacher? Where is she now? I'll tell you what I did with her and her education. I destroyed them both, so you can imagine what I will do to a person like you, who has no confidence in himself.

Many, many nights I cried or every night I cried myself to sleep. I thought about killing myself, but I was too chicken to do so. I thought about the ways I could do it, like jumping in front of a train or jumping off the roof of a building. I wanted to get off crack, but I couldn't and didn't know how to.

People talk to me and give me some good advice, but they are not the one addicted to it. I am. Today is another day and I am saying the same thing to myself: *I am not going to get high*, but the addiction has other plans for me and I do not know that.

All day I am feeling good and maintaining strong willpower, and an hour before I get off work, I am still keeping my mind off it. I am going straight home and locking myself in the house all weekend and watching some TV.

Ten minutes before I get off, here it comes out of nowhere. First the thought of crack enters my mind and then the feeling of addiction takes over me. My belly wants to reject the food I ate for lunch, and my mind rejects the good thoughts that I had all day.

"I told you before that you are my slave, so that makes me your master," the addiction told me. "All those good thoughts that you had today: forget about them, because I am here now and it doesn't matter what you say. We are going to get high today."

Now that my addiction has more control over me than I do, I do not know what to do about it. I start to stay away from mirrors because I cannot stand to see the way that I look. My cheekbones are showing and my eyes are sunken deep down into my meatless face. Every time I pass by a mirror I would hide my face or look at the ground.

This is what I have to expose so I can find my confidence. The more I dig, the more pain I discover. But that cannot stop me, because I know I have some confidence somewhere inside of me. But all I seem to find is pain and suffering, from a young child to a young man. I have to face my life.

I am going to lock myself in my apartment all weekend and watch Saturday morning cartoons so I can laugh or find something that is funny enough to make me laugh. Crack has taken away my happiness and left me with only one feeling: the urge to get high. The other reason I used to lock myself in my apartment all weekend for, was to lock up myself from myself. I put my ass in my own jail so I could control the need to get high.

All it takes is one to start the mission, so beam me up Scotty. I flipped through the channels and could not find anything that interested me on TV. And out of nowhere the voice came to me, and said, "You could sell that boring TV and get a couple of jumbos for it." I worked for two weeks to buy that television set and then sold it for two bottles of crack. I sold everything I owned and anything I could get my hands on in my mother's house. My mother started to sleep with her pocketbook tucked in her arms.

One night when all the money was gone and the high was wearing off, I remembered my mother's pocketbook. So I crawled on my belly like a ninja and grabbed the pocketbook from her. She grabbed it back but I kept on pulling and pulling it away from her. I could see the expression on my mother's face, but that addiction was in control of me and there was nothing I could do to stop the attack.

My own mother, my one mother. The lady who carried me for nine months and loved her big-nosed son very much. My addiction is stronger than the love that I have for my sweet mother, and I never, never had bad intensions toward her. That night will stay with me forever. The expression on my mother's face always hurts me whenever I remember it, like now.

I keep on getting high but my mother was losing weight from worrying about me. She never was safe around me and I was never safe with myself. One minute everything could be going well for me; the next minute the urge to get high would take over, and there would be nothing I could do about it. I was always weak and crack took advantage of me.

I am also sick and tired of getting high, but at the same time I love that feeling. I wish there was a way I could get high without the addiction. Then I would be a happy man.

It's been almost four years now and I have tried everything I know to stop, but nothing I try works for me. I am down to two pairs of pants and a couple of T-shirts. The clothes that I work in are the same clothes that I wear at night time too, and I am a dirty construction worker.

The freaks come out at night, so you can find me running the street at night. One night I went to the spot to buy some crack, but the spot was sold out. I went to another spot but it was sold out too. I went to all the spots I knew and couldn't find anything. I was running from one spot to the other, and behind me and in the front of me were about twenty people running too. That night, for about an hour, no one could find the spot that had it, and more and more crack-heads were searching together. Then one crack-head said, "I found the spot that has it." We all took off like the New York City marathon runners. About thirty crack-heads were running together all over Brooklyn, looking for that white piece of rock.

I usually got high with my cousin, who used to live in the same building as me, but he died, or I should say, crack caused his death. Every time he took a hit of the pipe, that would make him all paranoid. "Shh, be quiet. Someone is in the other room," he would say. "Yo man, there is no one here but us two crack-heads," I told him. I did not like to get high with him, but if he had the crack I did not have any choice.

Eventually I start to hear footsteps on my own and it's beginning to feel like everyone is watching me ("look at that crack head"). Paranoia has set in, so every time I take a hit I am creeping all over the house to see who is in the next room or who is under the bed.

Paranoia is the first step to craziness, and I can see myself doing the same thing my cousin did when he took a hit. *Lord, Lord, please help me get off this drug.* I cry every, every night about the same thing. I am on the floor looking for a piece of crack that I might have dropped by accident, but a crack-head never drops a crumb, Anything that's white and small looks like crack. I smoke white rice, white soap, and pieces of white paint.

I am a dead man walking, or a crack zombie waiting to be put in my grave. Here we go again: another night of crying and regretting spending all my hard-earned money in a couple of hours and having nothing to show for it.

I am weeping like a weeping willow and having thoughts of suicide again. But as usual, I am a crack-head who is scared of dying, but I am killing myself at the same time.

My mother keeps telling me that I need a physiologist to help me and that she just cannot figure out how I just cannot stop doing it. She wonders if I am just a weak person. To tell you the truth, I cannot explain it. I just know that I am struck in something that not too many people get out of alive.

Crack is a death sentence and I can see myself lying in a coffin. In the dream I keep having over and over again, I am climbing up some steps that are leading to a man who looks like the devil from the movies. He invites me to come join him. On the sides of the stairs are demons growling at me like they do in the movies. And on top of those stairs is a chair just for me, waiting for me to sit down and join his demon family. And then I wake up and realize that he wanted me dead so I could be one more soul added to his demons and lost souls.

What can I do and where can I go for help? No one wants me around, and if I go to someone's house, I get that special security look: "Crack-head is in the building. Crack-head is moving around. Crack-head is going to the bathroom." And my favorite one: "Crack-head has left the building." So you see what I have become, the worst drug ever created and I got hook on it.

My family started to gang up on me and wanted to put me out of the house. To them it must have felt like living with a rattlesnake that is very uncomfortable and very jumpy.

I am now down to no body fat—just skin, bones, and clothes. And my mind became just what the word means, no good for nothing crack-head. All my mind and body knows is one thing: crack and more crack. But the little voice inside of me starts telling me there is a way out. I thank God for my little voice, who always encourages me whenever I am about to give up.

I am sick and tired of myself and starting to admit that I have a problem with crack. One night I was getting high as a kite with my paranoid cousin in his apartment, and as usual he took a hit from the pipe and then started walking toward the back room, looking for somebody that wasn't there.

After I had convinced him that no one else was in the apartment except for us two paranoid crack-heads, he passed me the pipe. I took a couple of hits and sat down in front of a small table. He gave me a big piece of rock to cut into smaller pieces. Being a crack-head, I tried to be slick. I cut the rock into smaller pieces and knocked a piece onto the floor so I could smoke it later by myself. When my cousin left the apartment to go to get some more crack, I decided to look for that little piece on the floor, but the floor was covered with a very dirty rug and everything on that rug looked white to me.

I was looking around frantically, going out of my mind looking for my death on a dirty rug. I think I smoked everything white that I could find. I still couldn't find it and my obsession was killing me. I never realized there was a mirror over the chair that I was sitting on, and I was looking under the chair for that piece that I had hidden from my cousin. Sweat was pouring down my face and frustration had me looking everywhere, even in the kitchen, which was two rooms away.

I finally got up from the floor, and the first thing I saw was my reflection in the mirror. That person in the mirror was not me. I didn't recognize that person. I hadn't seen my face in about four years, because I was so ashamed of what I was doing to myself. I stood in front of that mirror for about ten minutes and started to cry and cry from my soul. This was not me, but someone else who had taken over me for the last four years.

I went downstairs to my mother's apartment at about six o'clock that morning and was still crying because of what I had seen in that mirror that night. I told my mother I wanted to talk to her about something. She asked what I wanted to talk about. I said, "Mom I have a problem." One of my family members said, "What? Someone is trying to kill you?" I said no.

Finally I broke down, surrendered to my defeat, and told my mother the whole story. Denial is the thing that keeps people like me on drugs for so long. I always told people I did not have a problem; I could stop whenever I wanted. Or I told myself that if I could get one more good hit I would stop tomorrow.

One first hit is the only hit that gets you high, and for the rest of the night I try to get that first high. Like I said before, the high only lasts for a couple of seconds, so I have to keep on smoking and trying to get that first high.

My mother asked me about going to rehab center, so I decided to talk to my union rep about it. I must say one thing before I go any further. I am grateful for my iron workers' union. After four years on crack I still had a job to go to.

The next morning I went up to my union hall and asked to speak to one of the delegates. I told him my situation, so he decided to call someone Aas soon as he picked up the phone I knew exactly what he was about to say, and he said it. "We have another one," he said. And the person on the other end of the phone replied, "Send him over."

I walked over to a different part of my union and talked to that person who was on the other end of the phone. He talked to me for about ten minutes, and asked me if I would like to go today. I said no very quickly because I wanted to get one more good high before I went. I told him that I was willing go tomorrow, so he told me to be ready by eight o'clock in the morning.

That day I went home and went crazy. I sold everything I could get my hands on and I borrowed money from everybody I could borrow money from. I believed that this was going to be my last high, and I was going to make it a good one.

This was a going out of business sale, and I sold everything for a couple of small bottles of crack. The last thing I remember was selling was my family's iron. I tried to sell everything except the kitchen sink.

I didn't realize that it was almost eight o'clock in the morning and I did not yet pack my things in my one bag. By the way, I didn't have much to pack because I never bought any clothes or anything else I needed. All I had ever bought with my money for the last four years was the only thing I knew, crack.

The next thing I know a car is waiting on me outside the building to take me to rehab. I pack my two pairs of pants and maybe about four T-shirts and the bible my mother gave me for comfort. I walk toward the car and slide in to the backseat. The driver told me that if I want to get my last high, he was willing to wait on me. I told him that I had just finished getting high yesterday morning and was finally satisfied.

He turned the car around and headed to our destination, the rehab clinic. On my way there I started to think about where I went wrong. That little voice in me said, *a hard head makes a soft butt*, and my whole family knows that I am a very hardheaded person.

I never listen to any good advice, so I followed the advice of the so-called cool people and I paid with my suffering for about four years. I should have told that guy who first offered me drugs in my hallway that night that using drugs is not a good thing to do, but I was so curious about the wrong things. And you know what they say: Curiosity kills the cat.

If I had nine lives, crack killed at least eight of them, and now I want them back.. I want to laugh again and talk to people again. For the last four years I have been trying to stop, so could rehab teach me or show me some different way of life.

Tears are running down my face because I am hoping for a life without drugs. This is what I have to go through again so I can find my confidence. I am the young man lost in the crack world. The more I look for my confidence, the more garbage I find. But I must keep on going until I reach my goal.

After about two hours of driving, we pull up to the place. It looks like an exclusive hospital. A counselor talks to me, asks me a couple of questions, and then gives me a couple of pills and sign me in to my room, or section B in the building.

After she found out all about me and the type of drug I use, I sat in my room for a little while, then walk into the kitchen and then walk into the television room where most of the group was sitting. I said hello and sat down. I looked around the room and saw old people, young people, black and white, trying to stay clean.

Later on that night our class—the beginners group—all meet in the auditorium for some kind of meeting. I do not know what kind of meeting this is, so I take my seat in the middle row, not too far from the front and not too far from the back. I didn't want to be under the bright lights, because I was looking bummed and was still feeling ashamed of myself.

Then a guy walked on stage and said, "Hi, my name is Joe and I am a drug addict." I looked at him and thought *hell no*. All the drug addicts I knew looked like me: broken down and busted. This guy has a suit and tie, so he could never be an addict.

Then he started telling his story about what he used to do when he was out there getting high. *Wait a minute*, I thought. *I used to do those same things that he used to do, but this guy looks like he came from a good family.* I was right.

He said he used to be a doctor and used to shoot drugs in his arms, and after all the veins in his arms got bad, he would use the ones in his legs. He talked about his days in a shooting gallery where he hung out. Professional drug addicts could find your remaining veins or the delicate ones that you didn't want to mess with yourself.

He said the only place he didn't shoot drugs in was his penis and that he could not be around needles anymore. He said being around needles reminded him of his drug days, and he also talked about the other drugs he used. I did not realize that there were so many different drugs and I wondered why would someone try so many drugs. All I knew was crack and crack alone, a ghetto drug, a narrow-minded drug addict.

I thought drugs were for the weak-minded people like me, or so they say. I never expected a doctor to say that he was a drug addict or admit that he had a drug problem. He kept on talking about his recovery and the things you were supposed to do to stay clean. Then he mentioned to us that addiction is a disease, like cancer. He said if you don't take care of your drug problem, it will take care of you. He also mentioned that drugs do not discriminate .White, black, young, or old. It does not matter where you are from. Once you try a drug and like it, then you will get addicted to it. Once you're hooked on it, you have a problem for the rest of your life. Some make it out, others don't.

After the meeting was over, we walked back to our section, where I spent the rest of the night in safety. This is my first night in the last four years without drugs, so this feeling is new to me.

The next morning at about seven o'clock, we all line up and walk down to the lunchroom, where I am surprised to see so much food. It's a breakfast buffet—the kind that is served in the hotels to people with class and money. I never knew that they were so many different things you could eat for breakfast, and I hadn't eaten a good one in such a long time. I think I must have gone back to the buffet three or four times and tried out everything I saw.

We went back upstairs at about ten a.m. We all met in the TV room in a circular group with a counselor. "Hi, my name is Miss Ross," a woman said, "and I am a recovering addict, and my drug of choice was cocaine." And then she told a short story about how she got here.

It went to the next person and he also told a short story about how he got there too. Round and round it went, until it got to me. "Hi, my name is Shedrac," I said, "and I need help. "What type of drugs did you use?' they asked me. "Crack," I replied.

Everyone told a short story about their lives and the drug or drugs that ruined their lives. This section that I was in is for people who had just walked into the program. It was something like a holding pen where they hold you for about seven days and then release you to section two.

The counselor started to speak and explain to us the way the program works. She said, "You cannot do this for your family. You cannot do this to save your job. You have to do it for yourself."

She kept on talking, saying, "You cannot come here because you put your family in so much debt and your wife or husband is about to leave you, or the system is about to take your kids away from you. No. You have to be beaten down, broken down, and tired of getting high. You must be tired of being sick and tired, and also have to admit that you have a problem with drugs.

"Admitting you have a problem is the first step to recovery, and some of you still don't believe you they have a problem. I know some of you are thinking 'all I need is a couple of days away so my job can get off my back or my family can stop pressuring me.' If you are not here for yourself, then you are wasting your time, because you are playing with fire and you will get burned."

I thought about what she said. *Am I here because my mother was about to put me out, or am I here because I do not want to cry anymore?* The blacks are here mostly her for crack, and the whites are here for so many different kinds of drugs.

This group meeting went on every morning at the same time and every night at the same time. On our floor next to the kitchen is the counselor's office, where you can speak to a counselor any time of the day and night. We are not allowed to go outside yet, because we are new patients and someone might run away.

Some people are brought here by their family for help, so they don't really want to be here. I sat by the window and watched the trees and more trees blowing in the wind.

Later on that day, I was called to the counselor's office to be interviewed about my problem. The counselor was a woman and she told me that she was also a recovering addict and she could identify with the pain. We talked for a while and she told me not to compare my story to the other people's stories but see if I can identify with the pain. It's the pain that brought us here, so we have to get rid of our pain. And the way to do so is through talking about it and not holding it in.

At one o'clock we all line up and head down to the lunchroom again. The lunch buffet is like a catered buffet at a rich wedding reception: all the good food you can eat. I saw the deserts and all of them were chocolate: chocolate cake, chocolate pie, and hot chocolate.

I was still satisfied with my big breakfast that I had this morning, but my eyes told my stomach "you can handle it." Before I started using drugs I weighted about 165 pounds, but today with this plate in my hands I weigh 115 pounds.

I was skinny and tall-looking, like a dry branch with clothes, so my eyes were bigger then my appetite. You could look around and pick out the people that were there for crack: the ones that looked like hell, the ones that looked like they hadn't had any sleep in about ten days. And even if an addict had on nice clothes, you could still tell by his or her feet faces. Your eyes sink down into your head, and your cheekbones shoot out like devil horns. Your face is coved with nothing but skin and bones. That's the way to identify a crack-head.

I tried as much food as I could handle and still had room for my chocolate desert. After I almost ate myself to death, the class lined up and headed back upstairs.

We hang around in the TV room and got to know one another. Some of the people do not know how to live without drugs and some want to live life without drugs. I regret that I ever tried them in the first place.

Later on that day we went back down to the auditorium to hear another person speak about his drug days and his recovery. He talked about the pain and the suffering he went through before he became clean. He also talked about the pain that he brought upon his family and how he lost everything that he ever worked for.

A couple of speakers came to speak about their recover and the things that they had done out there to get their drugs. Men and women all told a short story about their drug days and their recovery. And their stories all ended up the same. Drugs whipped their butts.

One guy's story hit home and made me think about my mother and the things I put her through and the way she was losing weight worrying and praying for me to get better. Tears started running down my face and the pain started hurting me from the inside out. I told myself the first thing I would do when I get out of there was tell my mother I am sorry about the pain I caused her and that the guy on crack was not her son.

You could speak to the speakers after the meeting, so I spoke to the guy who touched my soul. I told him about the pain that I brought to my family and said that I could understand the pain that he was talking about. I said I would like to tell my mother that I am sorry for the pain that I brought on her. "Don't worry about that now, but worry about staying clean and making meetings" was his advice to me.

We hung around for a while and mingled with the different classes that also came to hear the recovering addict speak. After that we all lined up like school kids and headed up to our floor.

Later on that day I went back into the doctor's office for some more examinations and some more pills. I do not know what kind of pills they were, but it must have helped build up the body.

This is my first whole day with out drugs, so I am feeling a little good about myself. Before I even know it, it is time to line up again for dinner. I am still full from breakfast and lunch, but this crack-head hasn't eaten so well in the last four years.

Now this is dinner. I smile to myself. It looks like they hired a private catering company to make dinner for the king and his men, and I am not exaggerating. I was absorbing food into my belly like an elephant drinks water. I had never eaten so much good food before, because food was never on my menu, crack was.

The less money I spent on food, the more money I had for my drugs on the streets. All I needed was a dollar for food: a fifty-cent cake, a twenty-cent juice, and a bag of chips. This was as good as it got. I wonder if I am in the right place. This is not a rehab; this is a resort and I am eating my way through it.

We did the same thing every day until we graduated to the second stage of our recovery. Some people couldn't take being in the program, so they left. You could leave if you wanted to, but why leave when we knew you would be coming back.

Once you have a drug problem, it doesn't matter where you go; you are taking yourself with you. A couple of people in here have been in more than six different rehabs, and they still cannot stay clean. Could I stay clean or would I have to come back to this place again?

It frightens me when I hear some of the recovering addicts speak, but I am putting on pounds like a bricklayer laying bricks. They know that when some of us came here we were beaten and broken down, molested and raped, sick and tired, hungry and weak. Drugs took away all of our natural desirer for food, so in here I guess they are trying to get us fat for the killing.

Second stage is also the last stage of my thirty-day program. We had more meetings, more group therapy, and more one-on-one time with a counselor so they could evaluate us on our progress. If they do not believe that you are ready to go home, they talk to you about extending your stay or sign you up for a halfway house.

Most of the counselors are recovering addicts who know exactly where we addicts are coming from. We started learning: Once an addict, always an addict. And that also frightens me. *You mean I will be an addict for the rest of my life?*

We were told that when we get out we should make sure that we stay away from people, places, and things. And this is my biggest problem. All my friends used drugs and all the places I pass on my way home have spots that I know about. I am still afraid of myself. I am safe in here, but when I get on the outside it will show up, because that not me.

This is the floor of reality and it scares me. We were told in meetings that not all of us were going to make it on the outside and that some of us would be back. There are recovering addicts who have been messing with drugs half their lives, and when I tell them that my drug choice was crack they look at me an say, "How could you? Out of all the drugs ever created, you pick the worst one." One addict tells another addict he will never try crack.

Now we are allowed to walk around the forest. That's where the place is located, so we could get a different thought about our lives. There were meetings and more meetings to stay clean and food and more foods to restore your health.

Some people who bring the meetings to us are people who got clean in this very same rehab clinic. So they try to encourage us by telling us what they do to stay clean on the outside. They all stress the importance of making meetings when we get out, because that's where the real test begins.

I love this place and I really do not want to leave it. In here I'm secure like a baby in his mother's arms. I was told that there is a gym downstairs, so I decided to go down and check it out. *Oh, this is nice. A full size basketball court, a hotel size swimming pool, a weight room and a steam room,*

After seeing all this, I went up and changed and came right back down for one reason only. I wanted to try the steam room and then the swimming pool. I sat in that steam room for a couple of minutes and then my neck started itching me so I scratched back.. Under my fingernails was a pound of dirt or mud. I started to rub my arms and neck and the more I rubbed, the more dirt keep coming off.

I always wondered why I kept on getting blacker and blacker. Today I knew why. The steam steamed my crack skin until it got down to my natural skin. Four years has passed and I hadn't had a good bath, so I scrubbed and scrubbed my whole body over and over again. Do you think being on drugs is easy? Well it's not.

I never took time to clean myself or feed myself, but I took the time to kill myself. Three weeks had passed and I hadn't thought about getting high once, to tell you the truth. The moment I walked in here, the urge to get high left me altogether. A couple of people signed themselves out because they couldn't fight the urge to get high, or the obsession that comes over you.

From all over the country people are coming to this rehab clinic to tell their stories about their drug days and their recovery. That's what it is all about; addicts helping addicts. So recovering addicts helping addicts to recover. It takes one to help one.

The speakers told us about the meetings that we have to make when we get on the outside. The meetings on the outside is an anonymous drug program that has meetings all over the country—in every state, every day, anytime. It's the kind of support group the recovering addict needs.

One guy told his story about being clean ten years and then start missing meetings because he thought that he was cured and didn't need meetings anymore. Again, this scares me. Once an addict, always an addict, because the attitude of the addict will always be with you.

He said he started hanging around his old friends, thinking he was strong enough, so eventually he started taking a sip here, a puff there, and so on, until one day that sip and puff could not satisfy him anymore. The drug of his choice was cocaine and it came calling him back like an old friend. Once that thought enters your mind, the feeling follows. The obsession comes in and takes over the whole body. Now it's time to go.

I did not talk to the counselor that often, because nothing bothered me. I almost felt like I had a double personality. I'm not that bad of a person, and I would have never tried crack if I was in my right frame of mind.

As a recovering addict, my best days on drugs were the ones when I was broke and I couldn't find any money. On those days I used to dream about life without crack and wonder if it would ever be possible to quit smoking. My good personality really did not enjoy doing it, but he was stuck and powerless over the other personality. Before the good personality could think about the situation and then give a good answer, the other one always jumped in and said something like this, I try it, I do it, or give me some.

Now that I am here, I do not feel like a drug addict or like someone who ever did drugs, and that is strange to me. The counselors told us about a recovering addict who goes around the country spreading the message of recovery, and he is going to be here next week.

His message is supposed to uplift us and strengthen us, now that we have about two more weeks to go. His name is Mr. Mich and his message made the whole class itch. He was big, tall black man with a very loud bass voice, telling his story about his heroin days. His voice captured the whole class's attention and also the attention of some of the counselors who dropped by to hear him speak. Right away I noticed his arm. How many holes could one man have in his arms?

He talked about the holes in his arms and called them tracks. It happened from shooting fifteen years of heroin into his veins, he said. It looked like his veins could not take it anymore and then they decided to explode.

He started talking about the monkey on his back and he is out there waiting on us like a lost friend. He said, "You guys are safe and secure in here, but in a couple of days you will be graduating the program and going back into the real world, where that monkey will be waiting for you and will test you."

He kept on going, saying, "Some people graduate, go home, and celebrate by getting high. Don't let that monkey trick you into getting high, so remember what you learned. That monkey is always there to tempt you by saying, 'Yo man, just take one for old times sake' or 'let's go visit our old friends.'" He said a whole lot more that I couldn't remember, but that monkey idea stayed on my mind all the time after that.

This monkey really sounds like my bad personality, and I know he is waiting for me to get out from safety. I spoke to one of the counselors about my feelings and my fears about going back home, where I knew all my crackhead friends lived.

One lives upstairs, one lives across the street from me, and I am nervous about that situation because I don't want to get high anymore. The counselor talked to me about a halfway house and told me I needed more time. I thought about it and decided to take a chance on going home to Brooklyn, where I knew at least ten crack houses.

I tried to enjoy the time I had left by playing horse shoes and trying to block out the monkey idea. I tried and tried until I got myself a ringer. Visiting day came and visiting day went, and no one came to see the long-lost son.

Last Sunday was visiting day and many of the families came to see their sick loved ones. No one came to see me and that hurt me for a little while, so I had to talk to the counselor about it. In two days I would be going to my graduation ceremony. from a crack-head to be well fed. I gained about twenty-five to thirty pounds, so I am feeling good about myself.

A class of about twenty graduated together and received a certificate of accomplishment. We signed each other's books and encouraged one another by wishing each other good luck.

I left the rehab frightened and nervous I went outside frightened and nervous , I went back to work frightened and nervous For about one month, I didn't talk much to anyone and I did not go anywhere but work, meetings, and home.

I was afraid to talk to people, so I bought myself a walkman and—you guessed it—a couple of Bob Marley CDs to keep me company. All my old friends see me, but I will not talk to any of them. I heard there is a bet going on about how long I can keep up this act of not getting high. Fulton and Franklyn is where I get on and off the train, and it is infested with crack spots.

Now I am doing well, buying new clothes, and giving my family some money every week. Hi she said to me, Hi I reply back to her. You look good, thank you, and then we started talking. I always had a thing for her, but she never paid a crack-head any mind. I am smiling at her, she is smiling at me and smoking a joint. She knows about my past, so she asks me if I smoke weed. "Yes," I replyied , because I have a crack problem, not a weed problem.

We smoked one and then one thing lead to another. Then I went home. I felt uncomfortable in the house so I went back outside to sit on the stoop. And out of nowhere my other personality showed up, or that monkey showed up.

The thought came and then the feeling pressured me to get high. My stomach started turning upside down and front to back. All that I learned in the program and in the meetings that I went to every night went out the window.

I got up and started walking toward that same crack spot, just like a programmed robot on a serious mission. These are the exact words that I said to myself while I was walking toward that spot: *If I die, I just die.*

The anxiety to get high is much stronger this time; that's why I do not care. My mouth started watering and my heart started beating faster and faster, so I started walking faster and faster. "Yo, my man,give me two dimes." And ran to motel that I used to go to.

After those two dimes were finished, I ran back and got some more. The whole night I was running back and forth to the spot. I made up for the time I spent in the rehab that night. I wanted more and more, like good sex, and I still wasn't satisfied.

I sold the two gold rings I bought for myself for two dimes. I also experienced that night the thing that scares me the most, and it came true: Once an addict, always an addict. It does not matter how long you are clean. If you stopped doing crack three years ago and your crack habit was costing you about a hundred a day, like me, once you take that first hit of crack, you automatically pick up from where you left off three years ago.

That night I got high like I always did: all night long to the break of dawn. That morning I felt so embarrassed when I was going home. so ashamed of myself. *How could I be so stupid?* They told us to stay away from any mind- or mood-changing substance, including weed and sometimes money. To stay away means to stay from everything.

I got home and right away my family could see it all over my face, and it looked like disgrace. They all ganged up on me and wanted to kick me out of the house. "We know that you couldn't stay clean. Once a crack-head, always a crack-head," someone said.

Here we go again crying and crying again. Now I remembered what the people at the meeting would say to someone who wants to get high, but it was too late. Call a recovering addict before you get high, so you can talk about it, not after. And that is just what I did.

We are encouraged to ask people for their number and find someone you feel comfortable with to be your sponsor. This person should be with at least a year of clean time. Who knows exactly what beginners go through? Every meeting I made, I would ask someone for their number but I couldn't find anyone to be my sponsor.

I called a recovering addict named Bob and started crying about the situation. He told me, "Don't call me after you already gotten high. Call me before you do it. Then I can talk you out of it." He also told me there is nothing we could really do about it now, but he would come by and pick me up so we could make a morning meeting.

Whenever you relapse you automatically lose all the time you have accumulated and start the count all over again. I had six weeks before

I relapsed. "Hi, my name is Shedrac, and I have one day back." People started clapping and clapping and then the speaker said "keep coming back."

We made meetings all day long and I told people what happened to me the night before. After a couple of meetings that day, I started noticing the slogans on the walls. Every meeting place had them on their walls. They read: *Keep coming back. One day at a time. An addict alone is in bad company. Easy does it.* And there were a lot more to encourage the recovering addict to keep coming back.

Things are getting a little bit better for me, and tonight I will be getting my thirty-day keychain back. I am meeting new friends and feel more encouraged every time I come to those meetings, and tonight a guy is celebrating his one-year anniversary. Oh boy, that's going to be me one day.

I like to see the recovering addicts with all those keychains: thirty days, sixty days, ninety days, six months, nine months, and the one-year anniversary keychain. That one glows in the dark. The speaker said, "Anyone here for the first time can get a keychain." The white one is for people with one day back, or for people who surrender to their defeat. "Anyone with thirty days clean [that's me] come up and get your keychain..

I made it to my sixty-day keychain and in two weeks I will be getting my ninety-day keychain, and that will be something special: three months without crack. Time check, anyone with one day, thirty days, sixty days, should I go off and get my ninety days key chain, it's only one more day.

Tomorrow I will be getting my ninety-day keychain, but today I have eighty-nine days behind me. I had my mind made up to get my ninety-day keychain, but things change. That night I sat on my stoop thinking about my ninety days, and all of a sudden I was under attack out of nowhere. First the thought came, then that feeling. But wait a minute. I am supposed to be a lot stronger this time, but then again an addict alone is in bad company. My mouth starts watering for that white candy, because the addict in me is craving that sweet tease. I got up and started walking straight to that same spot that I went to last time.

Everything I learned disappeared into thin air. My mind and body were overruled by that strong obsession, and it wanted to be satisfied. To be honest with myself, I didn't try to stop this attack on my mind and body. I did learn a lot about how to stay clean, but I never put up my defenses against the attack.

I now believe I wanted to get high that night. I wanted to experience that feeling one more time. They call that reservations. It's like a boxer who believes that he has one more fight in him left, but after tonight's loss, he is now convinced that there is no more fighting left in him.

For the same reason I knew after tonight there would be no more desire for crack anymore. I almost defecated on myself because I was walking to the spot so anxiously. With every twenty steps I took, I would have to stop and hold my bowels. I took twenty fast steps and stopped and held my stomach until I got there.

I rushed to that cheap motel spot around the way, like running to a long lost love. All my anxious feelings disappeared and my obsession was being satisfied. That night, as usual, I went crazy. Everything that I bought with the money I saved I sold at bargain prices.

I sold my 300-dollar TV with remote for forty bucks, and I sold my VCR with a karate tape stuck in it for two crack bottles worth twenty dollars. My music system, which I love so much, I sold for sixty dollars.

You heard about crazy Eddie? His prices are insane. Well meet crazy Crackie, where you can buy a whole entertainment set for under 125 dollars, and I will also throw in a free karate movie, *The Last Dragon* staring Bruce Lee-Roy.

I didn't feel so bad, because I knew this was my last crack run. I did the same thing. I called someone after I had gotten high. The person came and picked me up and I cried on his shoulder and told him what had happened.

He drove me to a twelve o'clock meeting, the medicine for recovering addicts. "Hi, my name is Shedrac, and I have one day back." And everyone said, "Well come back and keep coming."

After a while the speaker said, "Anyone with one day come and get the white keychain," and so on and so on, until he said, "Anyone with ninety days clean come and get your keychain. So I stand up and received my reward. That was a happy moment in my life. I finally accomplished something.

My ninety-day keychain. The day before, I was very nervous about that keychain. I remembered what had happened to me before my ninety days, when I relapsed on my eight ninth day. I passed the first test, so the speaker said, "Anyone with six months come and get your keychain." *That's me*, Clean means no drugs, no drinks, no weed, and nothing with alcohol in it, including some cough medicine.

It was only getting better for me. So the speaker said, "anyone with nine months clean." *Hey! hey! hey! that me*, so I added that one to my others. I walk around proud with my keychains hanging out of my pocket, letting everyone know that I'm a recovering addict.

The keychains are my trophies for my hard work for staying clean, and they all come in different colors. I have one more to go and that's my one-year anniversary. One year without drugs: I never thought that would be possible, but I used to dream about that day; free from drugs, free from pain and suffering, free from that four-year prison sentence that I got myself into.

At your anniversary you can bring a cake and invite your family so they can see what's going on in your life now. This is not a fly-by-night scheme so addicts can gain their family's trust again. N.A means, narcotics anonymous. Sorry about the anonymous part. But I must bring it up, or give N.A. the credit for helping recovering addicts stay clean.

N.A meetings are held all over the country and now in some other parts of the world. It is a non-profit organization, but we do pass the basket around so N.A. can buy more pamphlets and pay for the places it uses.

I meet many new friends at meetings, and on Friday night after a meeting we all meet up in a club that serves all non-alcohol drinks. You can still get your virgin piña colada with the umbrella in the middle.

Then the speaker said, "anyone with one day." Hey I remember my one day back. Anyone with thirty days and so on and so on. I was halfway out of my seat before he could say "anyone with one year clean come up and get your keychain." It's the one that glows in the dark—the one that represents the fact that I'm not living in the dark anymore.

My heart started beating faster and faster and my skin broke out in goose bumps all over and a chill ran down my spine. I received my one-year keychain and immediately tears started running down my cheeks. Everybody got up and gave me a standing ovation. Every time someone gets their one-year keychain, he also gets a standing ovation. It is a time of great achievement.

A couple of days later I celebrated my first anniversary, so I brought myself a big fat cake and invited my mother to see her son doing well. A few people spoke before I spoke, and they talked about when they first saw me and the ways I had gotten better. Some of them made fun of my relapse, but it's all good.

I got another standing ovation when I got up to speak. I could not say a word for about three minutes because so many tears were running down my cheeks. Then I tried to tell my mother that I was sorry for the things I did to her and I asked if she could forgive me for those things. More tears started following. There were enough to fill a bucket or two.

I cannot remember what happened next, but I have been clean ever since. This is hard. It is so very hard trying to find my confidence, the thing that makes me believe in myself, because if I had it, I wouldn't have been on drugs in the first place.

After I got up and dusted myself off, I threw out the crack-head in me. I decided to keep on moving on until I found what I am looking for, and that's my hidden confidence. I could feel things are getting better for me, I thought to myself, *If I survive my crack demon, then it must be because of the help of my confidence.* because I knew I couldn't do it alone.

So I shouted out with a loud voice, "Confidence! Confidence! Where are you?" But no answer came back. But a bright light came up. *I have found it, I have found it,* and dance my way toward the light. It's a mirror. *What's this all about?* I am looking for the man in the mirror. Oh I remember the '90s and my union.

In the mid '90s the construction business got a little slow with the economy and many men were out of work. My union also felt the blow of the slow times, but one thing didn't make sense to me. Every morning that I was not working I would have to go up to our union hall to sign my name on a work list so when work came up my name would be called.

I noticed the delegates that run the show would mostly call the white members to the window of their office and slide them in to work. But their minority members would get a sad story: "We are slow right now, but hang in there until things get better."

Many times I have seen white members just walk up in the union hall and a couple of minutes later they are going to work. I was out of work for about four to six months, and I'm a very good worker and they all knew that my bills were piling up higher then my stress level, and my stress was building anger and frustration in me.

It didn't matter what I told those delegates about my situation, and my unemployment checks were running out. I always got a sad story from those guys, and when I mentioned what I had just seen, they simply told me the guy had his family and mortgage to pay. *But what about me?* I said to myself, I have a family too. *What? This guy is more special than me? I do not think so.* That's what I should have said to those white delegates, but I was too afraid to look them in the eye and say so.

Back in the '20s, '30s, and '40s, blacks were taught by their parents to cross the street when a white person was coming your way, or not to look white people in the eye when talking to them. So our old parents started walking with their heads down, looking for their confidence, and they passed it on to the next generation and to the next generation and so on, and so on, until I inherited it or it was genetically planted in my subconscious.

Myself and about 65 percent of the minority members of my union were out of work, and about 25 percent of whites were out of work too. If it looks like racism and smells like racism, then it must be racism. one race controlling another.

Tomorrow I will go up there and tell those guys exactly how I feel, but I never said a word to them. I thought about what I was going to say to them all night, but then the time came and I would just chicken out. *I have to let them know that I am someone and I have a family to feed also.*

Frustration was running high in my house because no money is coming in. I was angry with my wife and my wife was angry with me, so I slammed the bathroom door to be all alone. I looked in the mirror and stared hard into my eyes and asked myself, *What is wrong with you? Why can't you tell them how you feel, or why are you so afraid to say what's on your mind? Look at you acting like a scared cat.*

I left the bathroom and came right back to stare into my eyes, pretending it was the delegate that I was talking to. Every day I would do this for a while, until I built up some confidence in myself. *Why am I so afraid of a mortal man who will die like me?* Dr. King said all men are created equal and death is the destination for all men, so he could not be more special than me.

My back was against the wall and I had nothing else to lose, so I thought about the '60s and civil rights movement—the way they used the picket sign to protest against businesses that treat people very, very unfairly.

My son was four and my daughter was three years old at that time, and my refrigerator was getting empty. I have the right to work, and I pay my union dues every month. So that Friday night I taught my children things to say, like Reverend Al Sharpton. "When I say 'no justice,' you say 'no peace.' When I say 'what does Daddy want,' you say 'a job.' When Daddy want it,' you say 'now,'. We practiced this all weekend until they got it right, so on Monday I took them to my union hall with the picket sign. My son had his lunchbox in his hand with the words *no food* written on it and my daughter had her bottle on a string around her neck. It had the words *no milk* written on it.

We walked around with the flag that read: *No justice, no peace. No justice, no peace. What does Daddy want? A job. When does Daddy want it? Now.* They all came to the window when the heard the noise. Oh man, you should have seen the expression on their faces: "I am going to kill this NNNNN."

After they could not take it anymore, I was called into the office and asked, "What seems to be the problem?"

"What's wrong? You guys don't know what's wrong?" I replied. "For the last four or five months I have been telling you about my situation and the problems I'm going through."

So we talked for a while and then I went home.

The next morning when I got to the hall and signed my name, they called me in the office to talk some more. "We are going to give you a job," they said. "Not because of what you did; because we have a nice one for you." I took the nice job they gave me, and said to myself, *All this I had to go through just so I could feed my children.*

Many members told me they are not going to like me for doing that, you know what I said back to them, I do not want you to like me, I want you to *respect* me. Find out what it means to me, R.E.S.P.E.C.T gave me my job you see, give it to me, give it to me, give it to me, give it to me. I am sorry, but I couldn't resist this one, so let me thank the queen of soul Aretha Franklin for those encouraging words and let me continue my job story.

"Please give me what is mine. I do not want much, just a piece of that big pie. I went back to work, and no one has ever had a problem with me since.

Now I am feeling good about the man in the mirror and asking him to learn his ways. *I knew it, I knew it,* I said to myself, I knew I had the word *no* in me. You cannot treat me like that or hurt me, and do not expect me to react, brother bob said, every little action, there, is a reaction. Those are the things that confidence will teach you.

I left that situation smiling and smiling with a sense of confidence. I finally did something right in my life for the first time. I stood up for myself. The loser, the weak guy is starting to believe in himself, and that's another sign of confidence.

The search goes on. *This is only 20 percent of my confidence*, I said to myself. *I must have more in here somewhere.* So I kept on looking. Who is that young lady? That's more of your confidence. So we talked and talked and years later we got married. My wife was the one who motivated me to take that first vacation and she is the one who always pushing me to take a chance in whatever I want to do in life, thanks babe.

"When are you going to see your father and the place where you came from?" she asked me.

"I do not know," I told her.

"Oh, so you are one of those people who abandoned their country.

One day (God is hope) I got the chance of my lifetime to go back to island that I came from, or as my wife would say, "back to your roots, Kunta Kinte." One month before I went to St. Lucia, I tried to imagine all of the things I wanted to do. So I lay on my bed and thought about it night and day.

I knew exactly what I was going to do when I got to St. Lucia: the beach, the beach, and more beach. I wanted to do all over again all the things I did as a child. I went to some waterfalls and sat down on a big river rock and blazed one, and at the same time I thanked God for my vacation.

I did everything I thought about doing and a lot more than I ever expected to do. St. Lucia makes me feel like the same sixteen-year-old but with a grown man's mentality. I enjoy the life like a child but handle it like a responsible adult.

Chapter Eight
A Grandmother's Strength

I'm leaving sweet St. Lucia tomorrow, the place that gives me most of my confidence. Everything I try and succeed at gives me more confidence in myself, and everything that was not so successful still gives me the confidence to try again.

I woke up to the crowing of the roosters on my last morning. Then I gave the Holy Father his time. Almost every morning I walk to the front of the house and pick some leaves off some tree to make my tea. Then I go running on our yellow-sand beach for about a mile or more.

Not too many people are on it so early in the morning, so I look back at my footprints on the yellow sand behind me. Some joggers and some tourists are enjoying the same thing I am enjoying: that piece of mind that comes from the ocean so early in the morning.

I want to leave and I do not want to leave. Why would I leave paradise and come back to the jungle of life where no one will say good morning to me or even care that I exist? I would prefer to stay in paradise and enjoy all my fantasies, but I have to see my family first, before I do it again and again.

Life means more to me now because St. Lucia reshaped my mind, body, and soul. After I spent a long and quiet morning on the beach, I left to pack my bags. Then I told my father I would be back. He said he know so, we shook hands and I left the island of St. Lucia.

I got back to America and told the whole story to my family and anyone that would listen to a good story. I became an unofficial spokesperson for sweet St. Lucia with my big mouth. If it was a secret paradise before this book, I will expose the beauty of the island, and that's a good thing for the world.

There are not too many places where people can go nowadays without thinking about some kind of an attack. It's a very shaky and unpredictable world we are living in. Most people have stopped going to big countries and are looking for somewhere new to travel—someplace where time doesn't matter and war is not the only topic, life is.

One night I got the call. My grandmother had just passed away at the ripe old age of 102. The root of the family tree had died and all that wisdom went with her. Her husband died in 1943, long before I was born, and she died in 2002. Her husband was a fisherman who went out to sea and one day never returned.

Since the time I knew her she has been a widower who lived without men. She never brought another man to her house and she never went on a date with one, but she had someone very special in her life and that someone was the man Jesus, who took away her loneliness and replace it with comfort.

For some reason I always knew that my grandmother would pass away after she had seen her last grandson. *Should I go? Or should I stay? Or should I go to her funeral?* I wondered. I had just come from St. Lucia and I did not really want to go right back. Plus, she had seem me before she died and that brought joy to both of our souls.

I remember when I was a child, every Sunday we used to go to my grandmother's house for that Sunday afternoon meal. The whole clan would be there. Grandkids and great-grandkids would all be there for that Sunday meal.

She did her best to teach her whole family the right way to live, and she also ran her own business and never worked for anyone else. She was a strong woman who had her belief in God and God alone. She never got sick and she never stopped praying to her God.

Every Friday night when the sun goes down. No one was allowed to see her until the sun went down on Saturday. From sunset to sunset she would celebrate the Christian Sabbath.

I remember the first time I went down to the island and the first thing I did. I went straight to my grandmother's bedroom, where she was lying down taking her last days of good rest. Her face did not look sad; nor did her face show any tiredness from a long, hard life.

This is what I saw: I saw an old face that said " I am ready to come home, Father, just like Jacob." She looked at me and I looked at her, but she didn't show any emotion or indicate that she recognized me. I sat on her bed and told her I had come for her bible because something had to keep her so strong for so many years.

I knew it couldn't be a man kept her so strong, because she had none in her life after her husband died. It couldn't be all of those kids that she had to take care of, because four generations of children could stress anyone into an early grave, but not my grandmother.

Every morning on my vacation I would go to her house to see if she would recognize me, but she still didn't show any sign of recognition. I always tried a joke to try to make her laugh, but nothing ever happened, until one day one worked.

She looked at me and started laughing and laughing, and then I saw it in her eyes. Her lost child had come home. This is the way I will always remember my grandmother, strong and faithful. She impressed me so much that I asked God to give me that same faith and strength that he gave her.

Most of my family went down to her funeral, and I stayed home to plan my second vacation back to St. Lucia, the place where I was born. Next time I am taking a couple of things to sell and trying my hand in business.

Chapter Nine
Business in Paradise

The time has come to do it again, and I can't wait for that plane to touch the ground. And the good thing about it is no one knows that I am coming. In fact, only my wife knew about it.

The plane touched the ground and everyone started clapping and clapping for that safe trip. It was around September 11 and people were afraid to fly, so when that plan landed in sweet St. Lucia the celebration began.

I jumped in a taxi and headed to my father's house, and he too didn't even know that I was coming. I called this one the art of surprise. If you tell no one your plans, then no one can stop your plans but you.

The taxi guy tried to pull a fast one on me by charging me too much. He didn't know that I had been here before, so I argued my point. The taxi dropped me at the bottom of the hill and a friend came running to help me carry my bags.

I made it to the front door and yelled out, "Dad, I'm home." He jumped out of his chair like he had heard a ghost's voice. "Is that you," he asked. "Yes, Dad, it's me again," I said. He couldn't stop smiling at me, and my heart beat joyfully from his impression. We sat down and I told him my whole plan.

I put my bags in my one small room and hurried straight to the place where everyone knew me, the ky' year. I sneak into that area. No one knew that I was coming. I sat down on a chair next to a little shack that someone had just built.

A couple of guys were playing dominoes in the place. That is the favorite pastime . I yelled out, "This is a stickup. Nobody move, nobody gets hurt." They all turned around and was very surprised to see me again, and my expression was just the same.

We talked with excitement for a while and then listened to some new CDs that I had brought down with me. The rest of my friends heard my voice, so they came to say "what's up" to me. The music sounded nicer on the island, so i turned it up a little more higher. Now the whole area could hear that sweet music, and nobody complained about the loudness. That's another thing I love about the island. You can play your music as loud as you want and play whatever you want.

Do you know that every Sunday morning when the island wakes up, the only music you hear playing is country western? Country music is taking over the island. I am talking about music from Kenny Rogers and company.

There are bars that only play country western music, and the people love it. Every day on the island I would hear this one country song over and over again, played by everyone all over the place. The song is called, "Let Me Be Your Stepping Stone." I think it is sung by a male and female. Country singers should look into St. Lucia for new opportunity, and if you do find some, remember to give me some.

St. Lucia, I am back to enjoy you once more and it feels like I have never left you. I didn't waste any time, because time waits for no one. And in America time is money, so I started my plan with no delay.

The next day I started building under my uncle's house. I was constructing a small store so I could try my hand at business. Two weeks before I flew to St. Lucia, I packed my stuff into some barrels and shipped it off so I wouldn't have to wait that long before I received it.

What's that sound so early in the morning? Just the rosters telling me to rise and shine, . Oh I love that sound in the morning. Instead of police sirens and ambulances, I hear the rosters crowing. Instead of noisy streets, I hear the sounds of birds singing by my window.

As time goes by I continue building my one small store and waiting for my stuff to arrive. It is the Christmas season and I am trying to open up for that time of money.

Every morning I would go down to customs to see if my goods had arrived. They have not arrived today, so I will be back tomorrow. In the meantime, the people in my area cannot wait to see what I have brought down from America. I told them that I have the latest styles of clothes and things that they have never seen before. 'So save your money," I said.

I got the good news today that my stuff has arrived, so I waste no time to go for it. Some people told me that customs will charge me an arm and a leg for those barrels. Plus I have a blow up boat in it.

I took a friend with me, so we hurried our way to customs and locate my barrels. They were all together. A female officer came over to check out the contents of my barrels. She looked at me and said, "They are going to charge you for all those things." So I started thinking to myself, *That's going to be a lot of money.*

She gave me the papers and told me to pay at the cashier. Then she walked away. My friend ran into two of his friends at the place with a transport on some other business. So he brought them over to meet me and introduced me as the guy from America who was trying his own thing.

They started helping me, putting back the stuff into barrels, and so I walked over to pay my bill. I am excited and happy as a kid on Christmas day because all of my presents are here.

I am waiting in that long line and my anxiety is killing me. An officer yells out, "The cashier is closed, so come back on Monday morning with your papers." I try and try to pay, and at the same time the guys are rolling the barrels into the transport without permission. I try a different section, but he tells me the same thing: "Come back Monday." But Tuesday is Christmas.

I walked back to the first section and realized the barrels are already in the transport. I looked at my guys and they looked at me, and then I said, "If you drive out with those barrels, I will pay you this amount of U.S. dollars." He drove off to the gate but was turned back.

I asked him what happened. He replied, "They asked me for the receipt." I thought to myself, *All my stuff is in the transport, and so there must be a way out.* We thought and thought about more schemes, so I wouldn't have to pay customs their money.

I found one guy who said he knew everyone who worked at the gates, so I flashed some U.S. dollars in his face and told him the whole situation. I stayed back and he jumped in the front seat with the driver and headed straight toward the gate.

Moments later he returned and told me to give him some more money so he could try again. They drove back to that same gate and I could see the guy jumping out of the van and walking inside the officer's office. He came back out and got back into the van and then came back to me.

"What's the matter, man? I thought you said everyone knows you," He said, "Don't worry, mon. I will get it out for you one way or another." We are in the customs parking lot, the place has closed two hours ago, and the guy I am dealing with is drunk like a fish. I am so anxious and stupid enough to steal my own stuff that I am willing to bribe a guy who smells like West Indian rum.

He told me he was going to try the opposite gate. His friend worked at that end. From where I was standing I could see the whole commotion, and this is what I saw: An officer pulled the drunk guy roughly out of the van, and also the driver. I ran down to the commotion, acting so innocent and asking what was going on. The drunk guy turned and pointed at me, while the officer questioned me and the driver.

They snatched his customs pass from around his neck and fired him right on the spot. "Sir, what are you trying to do? Beat the government?" an official asked me. "We are confiscating the van and the barrels, and we might lock you up."

My heart fell to my feet and all kinds of crazy thoughts started going through my head. I did not want to be in jail on a small island where a prisoner does not have enough rights.

We talked back and forth for a long time and then I was told to come back on Monday, which was Christmas Eve. I went back to my area, where some people were waiting for me with their money to buy from my barrels of goodies. "Where is the stuff?" they all asked me. I could not tell them the truth (that I made a deal with a drunk guy), so I told them that my paperwork wasn't right.

I was stressed out of my mind and there was no one to blame but myself. How could I be so stupid to make a deal with a guy that couldn't take five steps in a straight line? Why could I not just wait until Monday morning to get my stuff out? *Why, why, why, I am so stupid, . Now I am going to lose everything that I worked the whole summer in America for.* Before I came to St. Lucia, my wife and I brought a lot of things that would sell fast on the island.

Scared money makes no money, so I spent a lot of money on my idea and called it "business in paradise," but now it had become hell in paradise. *What will happen to me and my stuff—the stuff that I worked so hard for? Will they keep all my stuff and put me in jail?*

My head is hurting me and again. I feel so stupid: the guy who tried to steal his own stuff. Who could I talk to and who could comfort me on the island while I was so far away from my wife? I went home late that night because I was so disgusted with myself. I couldn't fall asleep.

Then I remembered the words of the Holy Father: "Why worry when you can pray? And if you believe in me, I will make all your dreams come true." Shizzle my nizzle. I felt better and fell asleep, but the next day the worries came back. I called my wife and told her the situation, and she told me God would find a way out for me.

All weekend I questioned myself. How could I be so stupid and dumb? Monday morning I prayed and went down to the customs building to deal with the matter. When I got there they told me to wait and then called me into a small room. I sat at a desk facing two customs officers, and then the door behind me opened up and two police officers came in.

The two customs officers started to interrogate me. They wanted to know how those barrels had gotten into the van before I had paid. I told them that after the female officer checked the barrels, I just simply rolled them out to the van. They couldn't believe that it could be so easy, so they asked me if I had someone on the inside to help. I said no.

The interrogation continued and I tried to make it look like it was the drunk guy's fault, but they were not buying it. The police officers in the back of me said, "This is a serious crime and it carries a heavy, heavy fine, and also jail time."

My heart started beating faster and faster as the police officer kept talking about the crime saying that they should have locked me up that night. The customs officer told me, "As of now, we are keeping your stuff until a court date is set for you. And if you lose, we are keeping the barrels and putting you in jail." But he also told me I could deal straight with customs or take my chances with the court.

They started debating what they should do with me and then pulled out the government law book to section 112-67-09-15 and showed me a very heavy fine. My mind was overflowing with shameful thoughts and the embarrassment I had brought upon myself. I hadn't even started the business yet and I was about to lose it.

"We are going to check your barrels again because we believe that they weren't checked properly," and officer said. And he was right. When the female officer had checked my barrels she just ran through it, and half the stuff was not seen. This was my biggest fear and it came true. I didn't want customs to see all that good stuff, because if they did they would put a price on all of my stuff. They took me to a room where they kept all the confiscated stuff that they took from people like me.

One by one they are going to empty the barrels and expose the things I was hiding from them. The first barrel is opened and splashed all over the floor while another officer is putting a price on everything he sees. And if he doesn't see it, someone else will point it out to him. So everything is being taxed, with pleasure all over the officer's face.

The second barrel is opened all over the floor and the taxes continue to add up, and this is how they do it. If the VCR cost 100 U.S. dollars, they would charge me 200 of their money, which is like two for one. That means I am going to be buying back all my things all over again.

After they were finished with all of my barrels and had taken seven pages of notes, I was told to go home. They said they would call me soon. I walked out of the place feeling like a you-know-what and thinking to myself, *My business is doomed. Tomorrow is Christmas and I haven't made any money yet.* The people in my area who tried to save their money for my store couldn't hold it anymore, so they had to buy their Christmas gifts elsewhere, but some told me that they could wait until January first, which is a three-day celebration called Square.

Two days later I got a call from the department asking me to bring my passport and answer some more questions. After I had hung up the phone, my first reaction was to leave the island and forget about the business. I have seen to many movies about the government holding people's passports and the hard time they have trying to get them back. *Now I know that I am going to jail, because they want to hold my passport, so I cannot leave the country. What should I do? What should I do? What should I do?*

If I give them my passport and the court finds me guilty, I may never see my kids again. But if I run away from my problem, then I will have regrets for the rest of my life. In fact, regrets are a big killer of the human race.

I called my wife and told her the story and the fear about my passport. She told me that if I ran away people would find out and make fun of me and if I stayed she would visit me in jail. "That's not funny, honey." I told her. But on the serious side, she told me to be strong and pray to the Father, and that 's exactly what I did.

One day later I went down and handed them my passport nervously. After I handed them my passport I asked the officer about my stuff. He told me that the department had not decided what to do yet.

January first, second, and third has passed and all that Square money had gone too. The people in my area couldn't believe what was happening to me, and I couldn't believe it either. I could see the disappointment on some of their faces. They had waited for so long for the good things I talked about so much.

I could not take it anymore, so I thought about my situation over and over again and then I asked myself, *Why did you come to the island? For business. And what does that make you? A businessman, so act like one.*

The next day I built up my courage and went down to the department and asked to speak to the person who was handing my case. Some of the officers knew me by now because of all that time I spent going back and fourth. So they were going to let the big boss know that the foreign guy was there.

I went upstairs and sat down in a waiting area; waiting for my name to be called. Right next to me was the guy whose van was taken away, together with my stuff. He told me that he hadn't been working for a while and that the transport was the only way he made his money. And he said it belonged to someone else. I asked him, "Do you think you will be getting your van back?" He said yes but he would have to pay a big fine.

The big boss who was in charge called him in first, but their meeting only lasted a short time. He came back out and sat down next to me and I was called in next. I shook the boss's hand and took my seat with confidence. I decided to let her talk and wait for the bottom line so I could start my negotiating. She went into a speech about the many different things that could happen in a situation like this. "But since this is your first offense, we are just going to fine you to the full extent of the law," she said. "And how much that is going to be?" I asked. She opened the government book and hit me with a brick, figuratively speaking.

"Is there any way I can pay this much?" I asked her. I showed a number her on a piece of paper, but she said there is more to add to that. "What more?' I asked her. She told me I would also have to pay for the transport to be released, and that price was as big as the first one. *Damn, they are trying to kill me*, I thought. "That's a lot of money." I told her.

She said that was the only way I was going to get my stuff back. Those two prices almost broke my back, but I thanked God for his crutches walked out of the officer happy and wounded at the same time—happy I am finally getting my stuff back, and wounded because I have to pay for everything I have left.

I went home and then to the bank to put my last bread and butter together so I could pay the government. I hired the same guys and we rolled the barrels back into the van and then drove off to my one little store.

We unpacked the van and then the news traveled that the stuff had arrived. It was time to make the money, but Christmas and New Years had already passed and so had all the money in the area. That day I didn't do anything but relax and ease my mind after that long, stressful episode.

That night some of the ladies kept bugging me about helping me unpack those barrels, because they all wanted to be the first one to pick out the best things. The next day, bright and early, I went to the store and started unpacking. Before I knew it, everybody was volunteering to help me unpack.

I loved to see the expressions on their faces every time they pulled something new out of those barrels. "Oh!" or "yeah!" they would say. Moments later they started asking me, "How much is this? How much is that?" I had not even thought about the prices yet, I told them, but they kept on asking me.

Minutes later two guys showed up and saw something they just had to have. "How much is this and how much is that?" they asked me. I just picked the first price that popped in my head, and they agreed faster than a guy who bends down to pick up someone else's money.

The whole idea of my business is to take away their money, but not all of it. My prices were going to be cheapest on the island, and I would still make a good profit. So far I had four people helping me and some at the front gate were asking me if they could come in and help.

As the day kept on moving along and people kept coming by to see, they asked the same questions: How much is this? How much is that? Before the day was over and before I had unpacked everything, I was surprised about the good piece of change I had made on my first day. I was also surprised about the support I got from all my neighbors, because I had thought that all the Christmas money was gone.

Things were getting better and the neighbors were satisfied with what they had bought from me. After a couple of weeks and after the neighborhood had bought all the good and pretty things first, the business slowed down a little bit.

I was getting to love this entrepreneur idea, my crash course in business. As time and more time passed by and fewer and fewer things were selling, I had to come up with more ways to sell those things, because my time was short.

I thank God for America and the things I learned on the streets as I watch the Africans drag their suitcases on wheels through the whole neighborhood, selling socks and clothes. I called two of my friends, a male and a female, into the store and told them about the hustles, and they agreed.

The next morning the two met me at the store, and so we packed things from the store so they could go throughout different neighborhoods door to door. The sales were very successful on the first day, so I made it an everyday thing.

Eventually my salespeople ran out of places to go and friends to see too, so my business took another nosedive. A couple of weeks has passed and not too much was being put into my pocket, and so I had to find more ways to make it. I called my wife and told her that business was not doing so well and I did not know how else to promote it. She told me, "That is how business works. Sometimes it is up and sometimes it is down, so take the good with the bad."

My mission was simple. I brought down the nicest things so the people would be tempted by what they saw and my business would be sold out in a couple of weeks. But this was not the case. Christmas and Square had taken all the people's money, and so everybody pockets were going through a long drought.

Eventually someone gave me an idea to make the business could start moving again. In the town there are people who sell things on the sidewalks, and in America they call them street vendors.

The handyman in the area built me a tray. That's what they called it. It is a flat, small table with a hole directly in the middle so that a big beach umbrella can protect your goods from the sun. I was willing to try any good advice someone gave me, and tomorrow me and my two helpers were going to open up my street store.

We drove into the town to look for a good location and we found one right in the middle of town, where everyone passes by. We set up and began to expose what we had to sell.

There was a guy right next to us who sells all kinds of hats and incense. His expression on his face told us that he didn't want any newcomers on his turf, so I tried to pay him no mind. After half an hour of bad facial expressions toward me, he started saying things.

I saw businesses come and go and heard many different negative sayings about my business. The thing about what he said was that he was not saying it directly to me, but he was saying it loudly enough that I could hear it. After a while I couldn't take what he was saying anymore, so I said something back to him. Little did I know he was looking for an argument. He talked and talked, and I kept on arguing back to him. My two helpers told me not to argue with a stupid guy like that, so eventually I stopped, but he didn't.

I turned my attention to the tray to deal with the people who stopped and looked. The guy in the background was still arguing and no one was paying any attention to him, but people were sure paying attention to my tray.

Things went nicely the first day, but the next morning the hat guy spread his hats all over the place so that no room was left for me. This guy is really trying to get rid of me, but he doesn't know I am a try-and-try-again type of guy.

I locate a two-foot spot in the ten-foot spot I had yesterday, so I squeeze my way in. The hat guy kept his eyes on me the whole time, watching to see if I would step on his old hats. It didn't take long for people to stop and look to see what is in my tray, without stepping on his hats.

He usually would say something to my customers, but they would say something back to him. He finally realized that he couldn't win that fight, so he removed his old hats and let me get back my space. My first lesson in business is never be afraid of the competition. "Location, location, location" is another key in business and I had the perfect spot. Everybody and their mom's mom passed that way, and so the street business was doing very well.

Every day the taxman passed my way to give me a three-dollar ticket, or should I say I paid three dollars for selling on the streets. I understand the system so I do not mind, everybody makes their money off someone else, so I must pay the man. *So this is what it feels like to be a businessperson, knowing how to deal with people and do not taking it so personally.*

Some people wanted to buy some things from me but didn't have all the money. One guy who didn't have any shoes on his feet was trying to buy two pairs of shoes for his young daughters and was short some money.

For some reason we started talking and then I found out that he had six more daughters at home. He told me today was his payday and he would like to buy two pairs, but he could only afford one and a half.

Business is about making money, but a good businessman knows when to bend, so I did. I made a friend and dealt with a lot of people without money, but no one gets anything for free. One lady wanted to buy something for a hundred dollars but only had ninety, so instead of letting ninety dollars walk away, I lost ten dollars.

Up and down, up and down. That's how the business goes. One day I made money and the next day I make pennies. No two days were the same. That guy and I were talking to each other and he even let me watch his hats while he ran to the men's room. The wife always tells me it is better to make a friend than an enemy.

I am not the only one with a tray out here selling things, but to me and a whole lot of people who pass by I have the nicest things, and all my prices are negotiable. I notice the other sellers do not negotiate, so their products stay on their trays a lot longer than mine.

From Monday through Thursday my street business is very slow, but Fridays and Saturdays are the money days. And if those days are slow I add a little flavor to it. Personality can make or break your business, so I developed a good personality. I was friendly to the ladies and helpful to the men.

My male helper and I would sweet talk the ladies, and my female helper would sweet talk the men. Women love to feel sexy, so we make them feel good about themselves and the product we are about to sell them. "This is the dress you need baby to keep your man in the house," I would say, or "This is the dress that makes every man want you. When you step in the party with that dress on, baby, all eyes are on you. I can see it now, damn!"

And the female helper would make the male customers feel good about themselves. "This is the latest style in America," she would say, "and all the girls like to see men in designer clothes. They think you have money."

This was too good to be true. A police officer told me that I could not sell in this spot anymore. So I asked him why not. "First of all," he said, your umbrella is blocking people on the sidewalk, and second of all, you are not supposed to be selling in this area. Why do you think that all the others are selling on the corners and you are the only one in the middle? So as of tomorrow you will find a different spot."

"No problem," I said to the officer. "No problem."

But there is a big problem. People know me now and the customers are going to be looking for me here. Some customers have left some money on some items that they want for next week. Moving my business to a different location means losing customers and money, and the people who have money with me may believe that I robbed them.

That afternoon after we closed, I walked around looking for a perfect spot but could not find one. I do not want to move too far from my good spot, because whenever you come shopping in town you must pass that way. The town is not that big, so you have one main route, and all the rest are backstreets.

We found a spot on a backstreet under a tree, next to a lady that sells cook food. The next day we set up the business in our new location and this is what happened. Nothing. I mean nothing at all. No money was made that first day. This is all part of business, so we must came back the next day. And the same thing happened.

Monday and Tuesdays are slow anyway, I said to myself, *so I will be back tomorrow.* To me the location is not that bad. *So why am I not making any money?* I am right next to the courthouse, where there are plenty of people who go in and out every day. I am also right next to the Derick Wallcot Park, where people take pictures every day.

There is a Catholic church right across the street from me that made headlines on all the Caribbean islands. Some guys who did not believe in idols or images of false gods ran up in to church with gas and their cutlasses, or chopping blades. They threw gas all over the people in the church, lit them up, and started chopping them without any remorse.

But I still cannot figure out why I am not making any money. We try and try everything that we know makes the street business move, but it would not move. After a couple of weeks of no action and starting to lose money, I decided to close my street business until I could find a new idea.

I came here to try my hand in business and put everything I had in me into it, so I depend on myself to make it. It is my business, so I have to make it work; no one is in charge of my business but me. If you put someone in charge of your business, that person will not take care of your business like you. Only you know what you like and the way you like it.

Days and days passed and I couldn't come up with any new ways to make my things sell, so I put all business aside and pulled out my inflated boat. Dreams do come true, and owning any kind of boat is my dream come true.

Chapter Ten
The Removal of Business Stress

Freedom, freedom, instead of business, business, and no fun. After weeks of business stress, St. Lucia's sky blue water is calling me. Whenever I am stressed about something, I just take a walk to that yellow-sand beach to ease my mind and get good thoughts back.

"Yo. Sean! Come check this out." I pulled out a box that was two feet by eighteen inches wide and said, "That's my boat." The instructions and the picture on the box told us that it could hold five people—three adults and two kids. "Yo, do you want to go try it?" I said to him. "Of course," he answered. "I ripped open the box and pulled out my boat, which came with a pair of oars that could be put together and broken apart like Lego. And it also came with its own pump.

We needed one more guy I told him to make that trip. Seconds after that a close neighborhood friend walked in. Excitement is in the air! And I could go anywhere. I could travel by land or I could journey by sea. America has taught me and St. Lucia has made me free.

Pump, baby, pump. Pump, homeboy, pump. I am excited to see my boat rise on an eighty degree day, and today St. Lucia waters are extra calm and a tempting blue. After it was all pumped up, we jumped into the water and began to row forward, but the boat kept on going the other direction, or its own way.

None of us had ever rowed a boat before, but we kept on trying and eventually Sean got the hang of it. We rowed out to a good distance and chilled out, enjoying the blue water like a rich man enjoying his boat. You should know me by now. I brought my peace pipe with me, so it was time to light one up for all the people in this world who love freedom!

I asked my other friend to roll this one extra big so I could celebrate the pleasure of being happy. *It is so peaceful out here,* I said to myself while puffing on my meditation stick. After I stop wandering about, is this really happening to me.

You guys check this out. I stepped to the front of my inflated boat and dived into the water and waited for the next guy to jump in. But they decided to play a joke on me by rowing the boat away from me faster and faster. So I had to swim harder and harder until they stopped and waited for me.

I climbed back into the boat and enjoyed the laugh they had on me. After we all enjoyed that joke, one by one we jumped into the sea, diving to the bottom to see who could touch it. We never realized that the boat was drifting, not outwards, but downstream. We started rowing the boat back up, but the current was too strong for us, so we let the boat ride the wind.

I was sitting in the front of my inflated boat with my feet hanging in the water. We passed right next to the cemetery. "I remember this cemetery," I said to the guys. "When I was young we never bathed in this part of the sea because whenever the sea gets rough and its waves came crashing into the cemetery, the next day you would find skulls and people's bones floating in the water."

The boat is being driven by the current and I am the copilot, enjoying my first day in my boat, sightseeing. Hey, there is a couple in the water holding each other so closely. It almost made me jealous because I had never experienced that style of making love.

I only thought about my street business situation once and quickly put that aside. With fun comes a new mind and with a clear mind comes new ideas. That's why business and pleasure will make you enjoy what you work for, but business and business alone will stress you out.

We started to talk about how we were going to get the boat back to where we started from.. "We may have to take out all the air and walk back," I said. "That's a long walk" said Captain Sean. That's what we named him because he rowed the boat the best. "It's about a mile back' he said.

I saw someone that looked like my uncle, but I could not really tell, so as we got closer I realized that it was my uncle and his wife, who retired in America and moved back to sweet St. Lucia. I shouted out, "Uncle! Uncle!" but he couldn't hear me because of the waves crashing onto the shore. Eventually they heard us and my uncle looked up and saw his crazy nephew enjoying his one life.

We rowed the boat ashore, where I joked with my uncle and his wife about their romantic walk. We still had a little bit more drifting to do, so we got back into the water and rowed out to let the current take control.

We got to the end of our drifting, so we started to row back to shore, where we could break down the boat and start carrying it back. God is love. As a hotel speedboat was passing by, cruising, enjoying the peaceful sea, we flagged him down. I used my American accent. "Yo, my man," "could you pull us back to the entrance?"

"Why not," he replied. So we handed him the rope that the boat came with. He tied it on and began to move slowly. The rope could hold, so he put the boat in a higher gear.

This is fun we all said as we relaxed and let the hotel speed boat pull us along, and then the rope snapped. We tied it back together again and kept on moving on our boat skiing trip.

We all agreed that this was fun and we had to do it again soon. "How about Sunday?" I said. That's why I had brought this boat to St. Lucia—so I could enjoy my Sundays on the beach, like they do in the movies.

That night I thought if I had an engine for my inflatable boat I could travel in any direction. Sunday came and we made that trip, but the rowing was too much for us inexperienced guys, so the thought about buying that engine was again on my mind.

Next Sunday is a big boat show and boats from all over the islands are coming to that event. And I would like to be there with my boat. Out of nowhere a childhood friend is looking to sell his two stroke engine to me because someone is about to sell him a bigger one.

Most of the people told us do not try that trip, because the sea gets rough and rougher in the back of those mountains, and it is quiet a few. Some say they will pray for us and some wish us luck. The trip is about eight miles or more in my inflatable boat, and the water is dangerous in certain spots.

Sunday is here and it's time for our daring trip, so we pack up and walk to the beach. After pumping up, some of the guys who were playing soccer gather around us and start making friendly jokes about my inflated boat.

"Be careful of the wind," they said. "It might blow away your balloon boat." Some of them started squeezing the boat and began to laugh at the balloon joke. Balloon, balloon, I am still going, so we put the two-stroke engine on the balloon and headed out to sea.

So far we haven't hit any rough waters yet, so I use my time looking into that beautiful blue, clear St. Lucia water. "Look, guys," I said. I could see the fish at the bottom. *Oh man! We should have brought our fishing lines with us*, I thought.

Now it is getting rough back here, and our two-stroke engine is pushing three guys against the wind. The front of the boat is not pointy but round like a balloon, so we do not cut through the water but fight against it. It feels like every time our boat goes five feet forward, the wind and waves push us ten feet backward.

We all decide that it is too dangerous behind those mountains, so we are going to get the hell out of there and try for calmer waters. But every time a big boat passes by, it creates a big wave that pushes us back into danger. Big boats, fishing boats, jet skis, and speedboats are all passing us at top speed, while our balloon boat moves as slowly as a snail climbing to a mountaintop.

We finally made it to calm water, so we kept our eyes on one particular mountain, which we used as a marker to steer the boat straight. Now it feels like we are getting somewhere, because we do not have to battle the wind and all the waves it creates.

Some hotel has built a platform in the middle of the sea and has anchored it to the bottom of the ocean, and this is going to be our first stop. We pull up and tie the balloon up and remove our weed. we put into a Ziploc bag and put it into the boat oar that could be broken down and put back together. With all those boats going to the show, the coastguard is all over the place and it just might be our luck that they come messing with us.

From the platform we can see our destination and boats are everywhere, and my boat will get us where the big boats are. St. Lucia is so beautiful to me that I need no permission to take my boat into the water. I just pump and go. I do not have to worry about the coastguard rules because I have my own rules: fun, fun, and more fun in the Caribbean's water, where the sun shines bright and the moon is such a lovely sight.

Just imagine Kunta Kinte away from the plantation on a dream vacation. Well that's me, so everything I do is a big deal to me. No one knows how long they have to live, so I will kill myself with the enjoyment of life. You know the old saying; If you don't hurt anyone, it's all right with me.

So I am in the right place at the right time. I never wanted to come back to my country with nothing in my hands or in my pockets after spending so much time in America. It is a disgrace for any West Indian to get kicked out of America with nothing to live on except the shirt on his back. That was a fear of mine when I was behaving badly. I have been suppress, depress, but never cold press, and still I wasn't conquered, so God gave me a vacation of a lifetime for my reward. So again I am in the right place at the right time, watching all those boats pass by. What a sight.

We gas up the engine, got back into the boat, and power our way through much calmer waters. We are getting a lot closer, so we approach the first boat that is anchored farther ahead in the water. And it has a foreign flag.

The people on the boat got out of their seats and kept a close eye on us as we passed on by. I knew exactly what they were thinking of, but it didn't matter what they thought about us while we were approaching their boat. But I kept an eye on ignorance as ignorance kept an eye on us.

At last I could hear the music pumping through the speakers while we made our way through the many boats anchored in the water. A trip that would take a speedboat half an hour to make had taken us about three hours, but we were finally here.

We pulled up to the shore and carry our balloon to the sand, where some of our friends were waiting on us to see if we had made it safely. There was a big crowd gathered in one spot on the beach, and I was going to see what is going on.

I chilled out for a while and watched a three-legged race and the egg-on-a-spoon race. I could have stayed and watched some more events, but my empty belly had something to say about that.

We left and walked up to the many refreshment stands that were made for this event. Fish, fish, and more fish: That's what the island is famous for and that is just what I like, fish on my dish. No fast foods on the island for me. So we bought what we bought and walked over to another crowd that was standing next to a stage.

It's going to be a dance contest, and any women or men from the crowd can participate. The women are up first and the men in the crowd will be the judges, so it's on and I am going to enjoy this. The men went crazy for the second girl, so the third girl had to come up with something that could out-do the second girl, and she did. Thong song came on, and she had one on and she used it properly, so you know who won that contest.

The men danced against one another so the ladies could pick their choice, and they picked the darkest slave-looking guy, who looked like he only know one thing, hard work. All the winners got their prizes, and I am about to go smoke my prize, which a friend gave me for being his friend.

I sat on a branch under a shady tree blowing my smoke into the leaves while I listened to some great reggae music by a Jamaican DJ. The sea breeze are blowing right through the leaves while I am puffing on my mellow trees, singing songs from the West Indies.

We couldn't stay long enough to enjoy all the boats and swimming events left, because our trip took us three hours and going back might take us the same amount of time. We said goodbye to our crew, who came to see if we'd made it alive, and headed back into the water.

Ten minutes into the ride, the engine stop working, so we pulled and pulled to make it start but nothing happened. There is a plastic bag wrapped around the propeller and we all thought it was worse than that. Everything is everything, and we are trying hard not to let the sun set before we leave the water.

It is much easier going back home now that the wind is working with us, so our two-stroke engine does not have to work that hard. We kept our eyes on one point and headed straight in that direction.

Things were going nicely until the rain started coming down. And then the trouble started. We couldn't see where we were going now that the rain had turned the whole place white. We do believe that we are still going straight, but there is no way of telling.

One of the guys is all paranoid about the situation, so someone has to speak some words of encouragement. He said, "I hope we do not crash into the rocks or get roughed up by the winds and the new waves that the rain brought with it." To tell you the truth, I do not know what direction we are going in, so I pray in my heart for safety. The rains are still coming and we do not know what to do. Should we turn off the engine and just sit here until the rain stops, or should we keep going? We keep on going and keep on hoping that we are going in the right direction. The dark clouds stop the sun from shining, and our boat is collecting rain and seawater.

Now we all are getting nervous, and that is not helping our situation. After all the guessing and wondering and stressing about where we were, the rain stopped and the sun popped its face back out. *This is good*, I said to myself. *We are facing in the right direction.*

We kept our eyes on one point, the place where we started from, and head straight to it. After we got to the shore and released all the air from the so-called balloon (the one that survived rough waters) we laughed and joked about the situation—about who was scared the most. And it wasn't me.

After the laughing and joking, we all agreed that this boat was not made for the rough seas but for lakes and calm rivers. So from now on I am going to use my boat for short trips.

You know what I said to my partners , we should play a joke on the crew that came to see us; we should all go home and not come back out until tomorrow so everybody might think that we didn't make it home. The next day, after I opened up my one little store (or my headquarters for business), some of the homeboys and homegirls passed by to see if everything was all right. "Everything is everything," I told them.

Chapter Eleven
Studying and Planning
More Keys to Success

Mr. Troublesome, that's me. One of the kids called out, "Can I have change for five dollars so I can play one of your videogames?" This is how my headquarters looked. After I finished building under my uncle's house, I needed more space for my videogame room and my music room, so I added a on to the outside without any permission.

One thing about the houses in St. Lucia is that they are built on top of columns, so you can chill under your house on a hot day, and that's almost every day. You could say I just extended the basement twenty feet by ten feet wide, and that was enough room for my plan.

Halfway into construction, I got a letter from my uncle's wife, who lived in another country, telling me to stop construction on her property. I called her that night and tried to talk to her and tell her that I was sorry for not asking her first but I could not stop now because I was almost done.

We talked and talked, but she would not give me a break. I got upset and told her the place was all garbage and didn't look so good until I came and did some work on it. "Now, if you let me finish building, I will make you a deal. All I want to do is use your place for a couple of years and then I will give you the whole place. Then the piece I added will surely raise the price of the house," I told her. I tried and tried and still couldn't get anywhere with her, and then a week later I got a visit from a guy who was the head of the building department telling me that I could not build or extend the front of the house without their permission.

He told me to come to his office so we could discuss the problem. I thanked God that I have a brother who was into the construction business, so I asked him what I could do so I could finish and face the consequences later.

He explained to me that if you have a roof done on the property there is nothing the department could do to stop you. I was going to face the consequences later, so I put the whole roof up in one day, and that was a good day.

I had one guy and a laborer who have been doing all of the work on my one little shop. But that day and night, almost all of the guys who lived close by came and gave me and my two workers a hand without charging a penny. And that happened to me more than once.

Before the roof went up, I had to get the concrete floor in, so I chose a Saturday to do so with my two workers. I remember that when I was growing up my father, who was a carpenter and his day, used to help one another when it was time to build their homes or add a piece to them. Money was tight and that's not the only way to pay for your friends. So they invite all their carpenter friends and had the women cook enough food and drinks for the helpers.

This is a time for friends, not my money. So I spread the word that I was having a helpers' party on Saturday. Saturday morning I showed up, my two workers showed up, and then one by one helpers kept coming. There were no machines; it was all manpower. Buckets and shovels are all we needed to get the job done.

We work, joked, drank and some smoked as the day went by so easily. That's the way I had seen my father and his friends do it. After we finished pouring the concrete floor quickly, it was time for St. Lucia's favorite food: green banana and codfish, or green fig and salt fish (that's what we call it).

That afternoon my favorite uncle passed by and asked me if the labor had cost me a lot of money. "No," I replied. "I used my friendship card." I must say they helped me out in many more ways than that, so I try to help them as much as I can and still be a businessman.

"Mr. Troublesome ,could I get change for five dollars, please, my brother "? Okay, I am sorry, my man. My mind was someplace else. What game do you want to play? that one he said.

My PlayStation is hooked up to the TV and the TV is set on the sleeper for ten minutes, so after ten minutes the TV shuts off. So one dollar will give you one game and after three games I will give you one for free. In business you must have a hook, and the word *free* is the best hook. I make you spend your money first, and then I give you something. You will not get something for nothing. That is not business; that is friendship and you have to separate the two.

I have three television sets and they all use the same remote ,two PlayStations and a Nintendo 64, and my own music is playing in the back ground. A main street passes right in front of my doorstep, so a lot of school kids use that street.

The new piece that I added to the house was separated into two pieces. and I left the front piece widely exposed to the street. So any kid who passes by must hear that good reggae music pumping through speakers and must look to see where it is coming from. Like bees to a flower, they started coming.

This is all business: studying and finding out what the people like and bringing it to them. The nose is used for smelling and on the island if the food smells good the people will come, and if it tastes good the customer will always come back. The eyes are never satisfied, so you put good-looking things in their faces. The children are attracted to music, and the videogame room is designed for them to stay.

"Schoolboy, go home before your mother comes looking for you," I said to one of my customers who only wanted to play videogames. They have a name for someone like that. He or she is called a game zorb, or zorbie, taken from the word *zombie*. It is a person who could play games all day and all night long. I have a couple of games zorbs who hang around me all the time. When their money is all gone they think that they will get a free game, but I make them work for that. "Go to the store or clean my place," I tell them, and they always reply, "No problem, Mr. Troublesome."

And so now I have a couple of school kids going back and forth for my one little store with many different parts.

One Sunday after leaving the beach on my way home, I met a young kid who asked me what time would I open up the store.

I told him, "In about two hours. I am going home to chill out for a while, and I will be back soon."

"I am coming to your house with you," he said.

"No," I answered back and kept on walking, and he kept on walking with me.

When I got to my father's house my father asked me, "Who is that boy?"

"I do not know," I said. "He just followed me home."

I went on in to take care of my business and chilled out for a while, while the strange kid kept my father company.

"Dad! I am going to the store and I will be back tonight," I said.

So the kid got up and followed me to the store.

We got to the store, where he helped me roll out the TV sets and set the benches up and handed me five dollars. He took the most comfortable chair and set it right in front of the TV, suggesting that he would be there all night, and he was.

Most nights his mother or father would always be coming to get him. "Go home and do your homework or just go home and do something," his father would scream at him. And he would complain, "All the boy wants to do is play videogames and hang out in the streets." His father would complain about this over and over again.

Three days had passed and I hadn't seen my strange friend, my number one game zorb, a.k.a. schoolboy. I asked the other kids about him and they told me he had gotten sick. That afternoon, as I was going to the beach, I saw him in his mother's window.

"What's the matter, schoolboy?" I asked. "We miss you at the game room." And then I started pestering him. "I am giving away free games every night, and some new kid said he could beat you in any game."

"Who is he?" he asked me.

"You know the kid, the one that took away your videogame money."

He smiled and realized that I was only messing with him, like I always do to all the young children I know.

"Mr. Troublesome, do you want to go somewhere with me this Saturday?" he asked.

"Where do you want to take me,?"

"To a cockfight."

"No, man! Homey don't play that!"

He smiled again and said "a rooster fight."

"If I am not busy I will try to make it."

"you're right," he said, and I keep on going about my business.

Saturday is here and this is a big hill to climb to the place where they are holding the fight. I finally make it to the top, pouring in sweat as I rush to buy a cold glass of lemonade, that cool, refreshing drink.

"Game Zorb," I whisper in schoolboy's ear. He looks back and smiles at me. "Did you cockfight already?" I said it in a joking way.

He explained to me about the fighting and the many different kinds of roosters there are.

"Do you want to bet," he asked me.

"No, not today. I just came to watch."

Many men are under a big shed, sitting around a circle like a gladiator ring. There are many roosters in the place, tied up to small trees, apart from one another until later.

One guy brings his rooster into the ring and another guy does the same, and just like boxers who touch gloves, the roosters touch beaks until they are mad enough.

"How much are you betting on my cock/" one man said.

"One hundred," a woman answered. "If it still works."

Just like a fighter, the rooster's ankles are taped up with an inch and a half needle sticking out for maximum damage to each other. Big money is passing by as the two gladiators are being dropped into the ring.

Roosters are jumping and kicking at each other, trying to push their needles into each other's head, and the crowd goes wild when that happens. Whenever a rooster drives his needle into the other rooster's head he falls to the ground and starts beating like he is having a seizure with the other rooster still attached to his head.

The owners separate them to let them fight again, but sometimes a rooster's brain gets stabbed and that makes him run around the ring crazy while the other one pursues him and ends his life. I asked the guy what he would do with those dead roosters, as he kept on plucking away the dead bird feathers. He looked at me like I was stupid or something and told me, "That's going to be my dinner tonight." I watched a couple more fights and couldn't take the madness anymore so I left.

I finally went down to the building department to hear what the man has to say about the piece I added to the house. He canceled our meeting, so I never went back and he never showed up again. I also never resolved the situation with my uncle's wife—not my favorite uncle's wife, but the one who was living in a different country. I never stopped building and so I finished what I started.

The videogames are picking up but they are not my main business, which is selling clothes. *What can I do to make the rest of my stuff sell? Should I have a sale? No, it is too early for that. I still have seven more weeks before I leave*, I thought.

There is another town that's called View-Fort, and it is located on the south end of the island. It takes about a little more than an hour by transport to get there, so I am going to take a trip down to that side to see if there is any opportunity. I told my father about it and he told me to go on the money days, which are Fridays and

Saturdays. I also told my best helper about it and he agreed to go with me.

Friday morning at about seven a.m. he met me at the headquarters. We packed two backpacks and two handbags of some of the nicest things left in the store to make that move. We took one transport into my town, where we waited for another transport to take us to the town called View-Fort.

I had never been there before and did not know what to expect, but you have to take a chance in business and seek out new opportunities to keep your business from dying. I took a window seat so I could enjoy the beautiful countryside. The transport came to a sudden stop to let a couple of cows cross the street. I smiled to myself and called it *cow rights.*

We pull into the town and walk around to see if we can find a good location to set up shop. This town is a lot different from the first town, and smaller too. The sidewalks are a lot smaller and it is lined with women selling all kinds of ground food and vegetables. We cannot go and set up someplace else, because this is the main street to all the streets and everybody who comes to town is going to pass this street.

This is not going to look right, I said to myself. *I'll be selling T-shirts and short skirts between mangos and green bananas.* This is not what I was expecting, but in business you have to expect the unexpected.

We found a spot in front of a vacant store, right between the pineapples and the oranges. I brought some hangers, eight nails, and some string so we could make up some kind of clothesline, and the rest was laid down on a blanket and exposed to the hot sun.

You can tell something about someone by the way he or she dresses, and here came a young lady wearing an outfit that make me think, *How in the double hockey sticks did she get in that?* The first piece of clothing

I showed her was the one that read "I'm easy and you do not need any directions."

She looked at it and began to smile, suggesting that I knew her style. *But of course I know you*, I said to myself. Easiness was written all over her face and her walk made the other women shake their head's in disgust.

The pineapples and oranges are selling and so were my clothes, so we kept on using our slogan: *These are the hottest clothes in New York, and we've got them at the cheapest prices in town.* Anything from America sells on the island, especially clothes. The people see them on TV so they want them. Everybody wants to be like Mike.

My partner knows what to say to the ladies, and today almost everything we'd brought to sell is for the sweet ladies. Women love to shop and I know that because I am married to shopaholic. Most of the clothes that I brought down from America were for the ladies.

The clothing stores on that same street as mine didn't do as well as I did on my first day, because I took all of their customers. So I would be back tomorrow. I went home and told my father about the successful day I'd had and then relaxed before going to my store—a place of comfort, a place of good music and a welcome feeling.

Game zorbs are waiting on me to open the place, and you know my favorite one is there too. After they help me roll out the TV sets, I roll out my big speaker box and put on Bow Wow and listen as they sing along.

Later tonight, after the kids are gone and it's about nine o'clock, I change the music to suit the older crowd. The Rastas and friends usually come out at night, so I play more conscious music while they burn their fire, singing and rocking to something good.

Every night after nine o'clock, I always leave one game on so anybody who wants to play can play for free, but this is only one game in particular and that game is Pac-Man. I introduced it to them, so every night there was some competition going on to see who gets the highest score. The game got more exciting when they imaging being chased by the cops. They are Pac-Man and the four chasers, are the cops who wanted to take them down. So my zorbs tried their best to dip and move away from the cops and at the same time eat as much as they could. It was like that almost every night, a place to do and see something.

The second part of the videogame room was where I chilled out and pushed the buttons to my booming system. (Remember I separated the room into two parts.) One guy asked me if I had the latest Jet Li movie. "Maybe," I said, "but I have some of the best old-school karate."

In business you shouldn't think small, because you will get paid small, and that's not me. Standing behind my counter, a place of private things, I could see everything that was happening at my one small store with many different parts. "Check out number twenty-two," I told him. "You will like that one."

All my videotapes are numbered one to forty and laid down on four shelves that are numbered one to forty. You sign your name in my book and the number next to it. One thing I should tell you is that after customs gave me back my barrels, the kept all my videos a couple of days longer. They told me it was to make sure I was not bringing something to stir up the people or brainwash the people.

Most of the people did not have VCRs at their homes, so I made them a deal. For an extra two dollars I could plug in this small TV/VCR combo set in the game room.

Some nights the guys would put some money together to rent one of my old-school karate films (the ones that I grew up on) or a live reggae tape of some of the best reggae artists from the island. The TV/VCR is placed in front and turned facing the street, where the crew is sitting with their backs against the wall for comfort. The booming system wire is hooked up to the TV/VCR so it sounds and feels like a live reggae concert.

Before I went home that night, my partner in crime and I picked out some more things that we believed might sell fast. On Saturday morning we grabbed our bags and headed back down south to see if we could have a better day than yesterday. In my one small business with many different parts, every day I try to do better than yesterday so that the mistakes I made yesterday I hopefully won't make today.

The ride is always nice when driving through the countryside so early in the morning, so I grab a window seat. *I hope the cows do not have the right of way like yesterday*, I say to myself as I hope for a better day.

This time I found a sweet-smelling spot right between the mangoes and the sweet-smelling island cherries. I had the same idea and same plan, so everything was going well.

At about noon the sun moved its shade from our side to the opposite side of the street. And now that the sun was there, all the market sellers and I were forced to find the new best shady spot across the street. I picked a spot right beside a clothing business that also sold good-looking women's clothes.

Every time we looked up I could see the owner of that business looking down on us with the shrew face. She was mad as hell because she believed that we were taking all of her customers, and she was right. She'd been giving me that look since yesterday, so she couldn't take it anymore.

"Excuse me. sir! You have to move your things elsewhere," she said to me.

"I am not moving anything," I answered with a rude voice.

"Well sir, this is my building and you are selling on my property."

"No, lady. I am on the sidewalk with all the market sellers, and I paid my one-dollar tax to sell on any sidewalk."

We exchanged words back and forth, but I stuck to my tax point and argued it all the way.

Everything went good, so we returned the following weekend and everything went well then also. This time I noticed the lady across the street was having a sale, so I smiled to myself.

Before the hot, hot sun reached our side this time, we moved some things to the opposite side and set up in a larger space. Twenty minutes later the sun reached the market sellers. so everybody was now rushing to the shady side.

It didn't take long before the market sellers started complaining to me about all the space I took. I argued with them about the twenty minute of hot sun I had endured before the shade got there. They made some good points to me, so I gave into them so they could have room to sell their carrots, peas, and the two live chickens.

My countryside business is beginning to die down, so I am having a closeout sale, so everything must go. Business, business, business. There is always a way to make in it. When one door closes many more open, so my closeout sale might work. People love a sale, so you make them believe that they are getting a good deal for their hard-earned money, but with me they always do.

One Rastamon always passed by with his eyes on a T-shirt with a lion on it. One day he told me that he liked that T-shirt but didn't have the money for it.

So I asked him, "What do you have?"

"I am a bush doctor," he told me.

"If you know what I mean, I am a bush burner,' I told him.

So we exchanged gifts like the old merchants did. "Another successful day in business," I said to my partner in crime as we flattered the lady who walked by.

Chapter Twelve
Sharing My Dinner with Dogs

Tomorrow is Sunday and I am going to treat myself to something I have always wanted to do, now that I have my own boat and a fishing gun that a friend just made me. That night I set it up and we met at headquarters where everybody passes and hangs out.

The islands have this fruit that's called a breadfruit. It can grow as big as a human head. When I was growing up the Rastas used to roast breadfruit right on the beach every Sunday. Thank God right next to my store is a big tree, so we pick four good ones, packed up all or our gear, and headed to the beach. We were heading to the back of a mountain, but not that far.

I was told that there were plenty of fish in that area, and I knew that I was going to kill one or two. It was my plan to gun down fish, catch fish, and roast them with our breadfruit and have a nice Sunday on the beach.

"What is that sticking out of the water?' I asked my crew.

"Someone's fishing trap," they answered.

"Do you want to dive down to see what is in the fishing trap/' I said to them.

"You're crazy," they all said together loudly. They told me the fisherman set traps in their nets for those who like to steal fish.

We had arrived, so we pulled into the area we liked and carried the boat all the way to shore, away from all sharp objects. We didn't realize that a foreigner was lying on the small beach getting his suntan on, because he blended in with the yellow sands so perfectly.

I grabbed my fishing gun and my diving gear so I could gun down my lunch and dinner. I always forget how to snorkel, so I drink more water than a man in a desert. *Here fishy, fishy, fishy. I am looking to find you. Come out, come out, wherever you are.*

I have been in the water for about half an hour and cannot shoot a bit to eat. The big fish are in deeper water and they hide in the holes of the rocks. A couple of big fish are tormenting me. Every time I point the gun at them, they all run for safety into the rocks. They must know that I cannot hold my breath long enough to find them. *Here they go again*, I think to myself as they wag their tails in my face, so I fire and again I miss.

I swam to shore and gave another man a try at it since I went in hungry and came out hungry. "Let me try the fishing line," I said to the guy I gave the gun to. And I started fishing, but that was not going well for me, as my hook kept getting stuck between the rocks.

My partner in crime has already caught three fish and he is pulling the fourth one in. The guy with the gun is not doing that badly, so he calls my name while holding a fish at the end of the spear. "Lunch will be served soon," says my partner in crime as we gather sticks for the fire.

This is exactly what I wanted to do when I bought this boat in a big supermarket in Brooklyn, and now I am living a dream. The breadfruit is roasting and the fish are ready to be put on next. The guy with the gun brings four more so everybody gets two apiece. Lunch is served and everyone has his own roasted bread with two fish on the side.

Afterward comes dessert, and I am not talking about chocolate covered in whipped cream but dark weed covered in white paper. We forgot to bring the rolling paper, so we are going frantic looking for some. "Let's ask the foreigner if he has some," I say. So I use my American accent. "Excuse me, my man. Do you have any rolling papers?"

"Yes," he answered as he turned his head toward us. "It is not on me, but I will go and get it." This always amazes me about some foreigners. He doesn't like people with color but would lay in the sun all day long just to get a little darker. And the darker he gets, the more complements he gets. Things that make you go, mmmm.

He returned with the stuff, so we rolled him one for his friendliness. We talked and I found out that he was from someplace in Europe and was enjoying the island sun. I wanted to find out more about him because he reminded me of a guy in a movie who escapes his country with a lot of money and finds a little island to enjoy his dream come true. This is not the guy's story (or maybe it is), but he looked so relaxed on the beach—like a man who had nothing to worry about.

We spent the rest of the afternoon relaxing, diving, and looking for that special sea snail that I talked about before. They live like snails, so you can find them under rocks or clinging to one. I did not find any, but I found some white sea eggs that I also talked about before. I took a couple on shore, broke them, and ate the sweet yellow eggs that are lined up all inside the shell. That's exactly how I like it. Raw, baby!

The sun will be going down soon, so it is time to make our journey back home. One, two, three, the engine starts running. Four, five, six, we had a good evening. So we talked about the day we had and planned to do it again really soon as we made our way home.

The next day I brought the gun back to the guy who had made it for me and told him something was wrong with it. He said he would fix the problem and take me diving with him when the water was not so rough and dirty. Three days later he came looking for me at my headquarters

"Crow," he shouted out (we used to hang out as kids). "You ready to go diving?"

"what time?' I asked him.

"Now." he said.

"Give me a minute so I can close my place up."

We are heading to a place called Pigeon Point, where all divers go diving.

"Did you fix my gun?" I asked him.

"But off course, but of course."

We pulled into a gas station and then walked over to a small bakery. I bought some cakes I remembered from childhood and a freshly squeezed passion-fruit juice.

Today is my day, I said to myself. *So anything that moves will feel the steel*. Last time I had been picky about the fish I wanted, but not this time. I was going to shoot at anything that was bigger than my tablespoon.

We got there and I sat on a rock with all my gear on and slid into the water feet first. He gave me a floating device made with a two-liter plastic soda bottle and a long string with a piece of hard wire so I could pierce through the fish and twist the two ends back together again.

I only had one problem diving around. I could not drag the string and shoot the gun at the same time, so I made a hole in my underwear and tied the string to the back of me and proceeded to hunt them down. *Not bad*, I thought as I put a hole in my first fish. Ten minutes later I shot one right between the eyes as it lay still beside a rock. *You thought I didn't see you, punk!*

After a while I picked up my head to see if my diving partner was not too far from me. I got slapped in the face by a big wave that spun and twisted me around. The string that was tied to my boxers got me all tied up as another wave that spun and tumbled me some more. The only other thing running through my mind besides getting some air was *don't drop that gun.* I didn't want to be the one who got shot by his own gun, so I took some more tumbling. As I rose to the top, the same thing happed to me over and over again.

Chasing fish got me stuck in a rough spot and help was nowhere to be found. The waves took my boxers down to my ankles as I still struggled to keep the gun from going off. Eventually the waves died down, so I swim my way to shore and took a much-needed rest.

I look at my floater and saw three fish on my hook. Three fish were not enough for me and my father to eat, so I slid back into the water but stayed close to shore, where there were plenty of big boulders that keep the waves from crashing into the nearby hotel.

This must be the fish sanctuary, I thought to myself, *as so many of them ran for safety among those big boulders. This is easy target practice.* e I shoot first and ask questions later. *Why are you hiding from me? Why are you afraid of me? All I want to do is gut you out, season you up, and have you for my dinner.*

I shot about ten of them in that spot. Then I climbed to shore, where I waited for my partner to return to shore. I sat there staring at my fish. *This one got it between the eyes, this one got it in his face, and this one got for not paying attention, punk!*

Not long after that my partner made his way to shore. I asked him to show me what was on his floater.

"Damn!" I said to him in a surprised voice. "You have about twenty-five big fish on your hook."

"What about yours?" he asked me, and then he started laughing.

"What's so funny?" I asked him.

"Those are the fish I cook for my dogs," he said and kept on laughing. He gave me four fish and a lobster off of his hook and told me to hide the lobster from view. "It's illegal to kill them so early in the year," he told me, "but in a couple of months it will be open season on my wife's favorite seafood."

He dropped me off and I walked straight into my father's kitchen, where he was preparing food for his chickens. He looked at my fish and smiled, but I couldn't tell what kind of smile that was. It looked like a "you did well, my son" look, or maybe it was a "those are dogs fish, son" look. I couldn't figure out the smile, so I asked him to cook some for me tonight.

As I left the kitchen and walked past the television set, the *Oprah Winfrey Show* was just going off and she was talking about canceling her book show because she couldn't find a book that could motivate her anymore. Miss Winfrey made me stop and think about what she said, and that made me think about the book I had just started writing. Now every time I write something with motivation behind it, I think about her and her viewers and fans.

This is what I will explain to her viewers on her show when I meet her in person. In my mind I have already met her, and my soul acts like it has already known her. And some of this book is written as a treat for you and your fans, Oprah. Hi, Miss Oprah, queen of the talk shows. I bring you something good to talk about and it's called life.

Have you ever laid in a river that runs from a volcano so your skin can receive the best natural minerals mother nature has to offer? Have you ever drank the black water of that volcano, full of natural medicine, to clean and restore your insides? If not, I have just told you about our fountain of youth, my sister Oprah.

Her words stay in my head as I lay on my bed thinking about how to get this book to her and her readers. After I wake up, my father tells me dinner is ready, so I push the big spoon into the pot and pull the biggest fish out. I sit by the window like I always do at dinnertime, where I can see the lighthouse flashing and flashing into the harbor.

Tonight I knew one of the tourist ships was leaving our beautiful island, as I could hear the ship horn blowing. Minutes later I could see that big ship appearing from behind the lighthouse mountain , it's the same lighthouse I always run too.

On most nights in front of my window, where there is a light post that attracts some species of flies and also attracts a pair of birds who do not know when it's bedtime. Iwould watched those two night birds pick out all the flies that hung around the light as a fish bone got stuck in my throat. This is a hard fish to enjoy. I cough up another fish bone. Now I know why he feeds them to his dogs, and I just did the same.

My father's coward dog always sits under the window waiting for food to fall off my plate, and after a third bone brought me some more pain, the dog ended up with a nice fish dinner. There was nothing else to eat and there were no snacks available, like it is in New York.

One of the things I had a hard time with on the island was getting my favorite snack or just going to a twenty-four-hour store. In America I could just go to any hamburger or pizza place if I did not like my dinner. But it

153

is not so in St. Lucia. Everything closed down at about nine o'clock and every family cooks their own dinner, so if you miss dinner you most likely have to wait for breakfast.

There is one guy who ran a small business from his own house. He sold fried fish, fried dumplings, homemade juice, and fried dumplings stuffed with seasoned yellow split peas. So that's where I went for something to eat and drink, and there are always two or three dogs staring me in the face.

Today is one of those dogs day, as I break off the fish heads and feed them to the dogs. After sharing my second dinner with the dogs, I walked to my business with many different parts.

Chapter Thirteen
Friend-Enemy

The place is quite and dead when I am not around, so things are about to change as I walk in my place. Besides the regular crowd waiting on me, there is a guy who forgot to get his girlfriend a birthday present. "Hi," he says to me, and he asks me to show him the things I have for women.

When the videogame room is open, video rental is available, and the clothing department is open too. This is my one small business with many different parts. He walks around the clothing department to see if anything catches his eyes, and he finds two that do.

A red teddy and a pink lteddy are hanging up in the player section, where all the name brands and nice clothes are. I didn't try to convince him to buy anything, because his mind was full with fantasies and his face reacted with a smile.

"Plastic or brown bag?" I asked him. "It does not matter." he replied. I folded up his purchase and handed it to him in a small black plastic bag. Now that he was another satisfied customer, I headed over to deal with two more customers who wanted to swap some of their own paintings for a couple of my CDs. I made that deal, hung out for a while, and then headed back to my father's house.

On my way home my belly started bothering me. Mother nature was calling and I hated to use that outhouse. Out of all the houses on the hill, my father's house is the only one without indoor plumbing. That's why I choose the tree every morning.

America has spoiled me with the luxury of indoor plumbing, so it is hard to get used to the outdoor kind. Plus there is a mother hen and her chicks who sleep there at nighttime, and she is very protective. And also the frogs come in for shelter in the dark corners, and I am petrified of island frogs with those big fat ticks on their backs.

I couldn't get used to it. It didn't matter what comfortable bathroom I was thinking of, because that hard old wooden seat kept on giving me splinters. Eventually I couldn't take so many splinters, so I hired a childhood friend to build my father an indoor bathroom. Now he is happy and I am happier to do my business in a comfortable place.

Things are going very well with my videogames, as school kids keep bringing their friends to the flavor of the month, my place. I had a very fortunate day in videogames, and I hope tomorrow will be better or just the same. The next morning I am still feeling good about all those school kids coming to my place now, but today is not yesterday.

After about three minutes in my store I realize one of my windows was broken into. I panic and look around to see what is missing besides all my videogame. and then rush over to see if my entertainment system is missing and my heart drops to the floor as I see the entertainment system is still there. After I look around to see what else is missing, the first person who pops into my head is a guy I consider a good friend, but I immediately brush that aside.

The neighbors heard about the situation and came over to find out what was taken. Some of the neighbors who always passed by the store pointed out something to me: The person who broke through the window was a small person, and the person knew exactly what he wanted and knew how I set my things up. I knew that person knew my place, because he took his time to unwrap the black tape from all the wires that held the connecters together.

Some people know my business too well, as one person pointed out to me that two name-brand sweat suits were missing from the player's section. Also missing were men's cologne and a couple pairs of T-shirts.

We debated and debated about the clues and figured out it was someone close to me, but whom? They told me to make a police report, so I went down town to do so. I talked to two officers as they took down my words.

"Do you know the serial numbers of the things that are missing?" they asked me.

"No, I never took them down."

"Okay, did you mark your items in any way so you could identify them if you see them?"

"No," I answered again.

"All right," they said, ?let's take a ride to your place so we can see the crime scene."

At my place the detectives went over the broken window and figured out it was someone small, like one of those school kids. After their short investigation of my place, they gave me their card and told me to call them if I found out anything.

I am furious about the situation now that I have lost a big part of my business. I reminisce about yesterday being my best day in videogames as the money came in. Chi-ching, chi-ching, chi-ching. You should have seen it. School kids brought their friends as I put on the latest hip hop music, and showed some of them how to stand in a B-boy stands and nod their heads back and forth to the music.

Now everybody is wondering why I didn't put the burglar bars on my windows. Procrastination and getting too comfortable caused my place to get robbed.

After I had finished building the place, I bought some aluminum louver windows and thought to myself, *That will be good enough until I decide to put bars in.* I had had the money and the time to do it, but I didn't do it. In fact, I let my guard down and let some people get close to me as friends. Now I would be forced to put the burglar bars in to protect the rest of my stuff.

The videogames were my back up in my business, and so was the face of my business. In my business plans I knew that the clothes would not be selling like hot cakes, and so the videogames were brought in to pick up the slack. I asked someone to go to get the burglar bar maker and tell him it was an emergency. We talked about the situation and whether he could make me burglar bars for all the windows tonight. He told me he could only finish one for today and would finish the rest tomorrow. "That's not comforting news," I told him. "What if the person comes back tonight to finish the job."

The news was all over the neighborhood that my place had been robbed. "Someone has broken into Crow's nest," people said. The school kids would be coming soon to play and listen to some of their favorite music. Here they came now. "Where are the games?" they all asked me.

"Somebody robbed me," I told them as they stood there looking lost.

He had made that one burglar bar to protect my busted window, but I was still very nervous about the unprotected windows. Two of my associates volunteered to spend the night in my store as security to protect my place with machetes. That night I went home stressed and unsure about what to do. Should I close down and leave? Or should I stay? I knew that the clothes were not selling too well nowadays, and it was the videogames that was carrying the load. And all evidence was pointing to someone close to me, but whom?

I talked to my wife again and asked her how fast she could ship me new videogames and some of my favorite American snacks, the kind I couldn't find in the island stores. Days and days passed and no one could tell me who had broken into my store, but they all said that someone I knew had set me up.

The area is a small area, so everybody know one another and now evidence was pointing at one of them. One of my game zorbs told me to take a close look at one guy, and then in time I started noticing he had just bought himself a small but expensive radio and a couple pairs of shorts. In every ghetto or poor place in the world you can tell when someone has just come into some money and that is the why I thought it was him, but I was wrong.

My place is dead now, and most of my game zorb kids are now back running the streets. My place is a place I wish someone had when I was growing up, a place where I would have been every day, playing games and listening to some good music. I never predicted this could have happened to me in business. It was a major setback to me again.

In my plan and dreams it was easy as one, two, three. I would come and make all the money and then leave the place with a pocketful, but now my dreams were a reality and nightmares came with them.

If I sell a T-shirt a week I am doing well, but I am not. The person who robbed me is hurting my business and that hurts my pockets. The only thing I have going for me right now is the weekend country trips.

I called my wife out of frustration and asked her why it was taking her so long for my stuff to get here. She told me the boat had just left and it was going to take two more weeks. "Two more weeks," I yelled at her. Some of the school kids passed by to ask when the new games were coming, and I told them they would arrive soon.

Sometime later a friend came to me with a riddle. "Riddle me this and riddle me that, black man. Someone you are really close to, someone who, from what I see, you treat very well. Oh and one more thing: You and that person go way back." And then he left it at that.

That night I tried to figure out who that person was but I could not. *Could it be my partner in crime, or could it be Captain Sean, the one who loves my balloon boat? Both of them know my operation inside and out, but those older guys would have gone for the entertainment system first because it's worth a lot more money.* On the island, one of the most expensive things to buy is musical components and it is so easy to sell stolen parts.

Time reveals all secrets, so someone else dropped some more information on me about this person and I was surprised but not shocked. The first person that had come to my mind when I first learned of the burglary was that person, but I refused to believe it. It's like someone telling you about your no-good mate but you won't believe it or you are too blind to see what is going on.

I called him Jealous, and that's exactly what I will call him. The very first time I met Jealous he asked me about my clothes and told me how much he loved the style, so from then on we started to talk about the store I wanted to open up. "I could used a face like yours to help promote the place,' I had told him. He is from the hip hop generation and the girls are very attracted to him, so I was going to use him to attract the young ladies to my place.

Before I left St. Lucia the first time, I made sure I gave him most of my clothes and the pair of boots that he loved to see on my feet so he could be the best-dressed kid on his block. It is no secret that black people love clothes and love to look good, so I helped him out. When I came back down to St. Lucia, he was the one who was helping me at customs, when I was busted. He was the one I would basically let run the place when something else came up.

Jealous had cooking skills and whenever he made something new he brought me a piece to try. He was the only one that could play free videogames and play with my entertainment system, like a good friend.

I could get one of the guys to give him a beat down, or I could just call the cops on my so-called friend. The funny part about it is I know his family and they know he looks up to me, and his mother is always glad to see her boy around the store, because she knows her young son is safe in my place.

No money is being made because of this guy, and my conscience is telling me to deal with him in a different way, but how? Silence is deadly, so that's what I am going to use against my friend-enemy. While I am thinking about what to do about my friend-enemy, my stuff comes and another funny thing about it is the stuff had been put in his mother's name, because she knows someone who knows someone who could get my stuff out of customs easily.

Thank God my stuff is here and my wife also sent me some new items to keep the business moving, along with some of my favorite American snacks. I hang up the new stuff and roll out the brand new games with a smile on my face, saying to myself I am back in business again.

Now it's time to let the school kids know that the videogames are here, so I walk down to the junction where all the school kids from different schools pass through. My store is about four houses away from the junction and I have the right product for the right environment, new games for the school kids.

As the day progressed and some kids pass by, the place felt like the old place again. Here came my friend-enemy, coming to play a game. *Should I tell him he cannot come to my place or should I get in his face with my argument?*

"What's up?" I said to him.

"I came to check out the new games," he said as he tried to walk in like he used to.

"Hold on," I said to him. "I will bring them for you to see."

He looked at me like he was surprised.

He picked one. As I put out my hand for my dollar, he looked surprised again. After his game went off he sat there waiting for me to turn it back on, but I said, "If you're playing. pay. But if you're not, someone else wants to play." He got up and stood around for a short time and then left, I guess he felt uncomfortable around me. I never stopped him from coming to my store, but he couldn't do the things he used to do at my place.

Sometimes he would bring me something to try and I always refused by telling him I had had enough of that. If he said hi to me I answered back, but that was it. We were friends but now I am giving him a very cold shoulder, and I see the results whenever he comes to my place.

Sometimes I see my friend-enemy hesitating to come to my place and I say to myself, *It must be guilt eating at his insides.* I hope you do not think I am a fool to let him go, but every time he sees me his head drops to the ground in shame, and my head is held up high like a flag, and that's why. Silence is deadly. He thinks I know but doesn't know what I know, so he does not know what I will do and that has him nervous and very uneasy around me. One more thing I must say is to keep one eye on your enemies and both eyes on your so-called friends. Eventually Jealous faded away from me, so he does not come to my place anymore.

Chapter Fourteen
Back in Business

Back to business. Old things sprinkled with new things make my business spice up again. I remember the officer from the first town telling me I could not sell in this area from Monday through Thursday, but on Friday and Saturday everyone could sell on that main street. On Friday morning my partner in crime and I packed two bags mixed with old and new things and headed back to our town, right next to the guy with all those old hats.

I nodded my head to him, so he nodded his head back to me. We spread the stuff all over the street and some clothes were hung up on the umbrella. We didn't have to wait that long for the passersby to stop and look, as many of them did. 'What happened to you?' some old customers said to me. "I had to reorganize my business," I answered them.

In my crash course in business I learned a couple of things: Always keep your business fresh by renewing it over and over again. People get tired of seeing the same stuff all the time, but the new and the old together does not look that bad.

This is the kind of feeling I like to feel. I am making money on an idea on a tropical island, I said to myself. I do not like to share my ideas with too many people, because someone always has something to say. "This is not going to work," they say. Or "If it were me I would not spend my money on that stupid idea." And the more you listen to that, the more you start doubting yourself. It's like that old saying goes: Loose lips sink ships.

So I keep my ideas and boat afloat with the things I don't say. But I must confess that business is where it's at.

All my life I have been working for people, making someone else rich and richer. I was wondering when I would ever get my break as I sold some young lady a skintight suit. That is the first style of clothing young women are drawn to as they look through the sleazy and pick out the sleaziest.

Here comes meals on wheels, the guy who sells food and drinks on his homemade pushcart.

"Long time no see," I said.

"Same to you," he replied.

"What do you have today, sir?"

"The usual," he answered.

"What is in the small bucket?' I asked him.

"Blood pudding," he told me.

Never will I ever eat that again. I remember I used to eat that as a child growing up. Every Christmas my father or his friends would kill a pig for celebration. After stabbing the pig in his neck and letting all the blood drain into a bucket, someone would add some seasoning to the blood and then pour the seasoned blood into the gutted pig's intestine. Then that would be put into a pot for boiling and then eaten with a lot of West Indian hot sauce.

"I will have the fish dinner and my partner the same," I said to him. We could not enjoy our food because people were stopping to check out what caught their eyes. My partner told me that our shopping bags are almost gone, so I walk across the street to a store the people call Chinatown.

It is not like the big cities in the world, so I smile to myself as I walk on in. I see four Chinese people and some hired help running this big department store the people call Chinatown. And do you know that they sell everything? If you cannot find it here or there, you can always find it in a place called Chinatown, in a city near you. They only have one store now, but after one came two.

There are also Jews, Arabians, and Americans doing business on the sweet island of St. Lucia. I bought what I bought and headed back to my small business, and I am not ashamed of selling clothes on the sidewalk. All big businesses start small and then grow into something big. And this makes me work harder and harder for myself, and one day I will have what I work so hard for.

Some business-minded people hired a local DJ to promote their product, so I have sweet reggae playing in my background and that turns me and my partner on to sell more. Music calms the savage beast and also releases the stress of this world because you can dance to it, so I am rejuvenated to sell, and sell I do. I went home that night feeling good about my comeback, so I thanked my Lord for this good day I had in business. It's snack time and that's what the neighborhood is bugging me about. "Crow, you are in the wrong business." That's what the people say. . As they try to flatter me into giving them one more.

Those are my favorite snacks that my sweet wife shipped down to me in a country that does not carry my favorite snacks. "You could sell those snacks and make a lot of money," the people told me as they tried many different ways to make me give them up. "Oh, that's not bad idea," I said as I thought about it for a moment. *Maybe one day*, I said to myself. In business every idea needs to be checked out first instead of just being dismissed. My old man was no different by the way he ran through the ones I gave him, and the rest I kept in private.

Every night after dinner I would carry one in my pocket so I could enjoy it in my store, but tonight I stopped and chilled with the young boys on the corner. It was the same corner where I used to chill out with my friends when I was growing up. Although things change, they still remain the same. The young boys talk about girls, girls, clothes, and more girls.

On that wall we all sat and dreamed about making it rich, the things we would do with the money, and helping the poor. And you know what? My dreams are still the same I am still going to help the poor.

I could still see a couple of letters of my name tattooed on that wall. After a very close examination and I also saw some of the old crew's names. I was very fortunate to see some of my old friends again, just like a twenty-year high school reunion.

The one friend I really wanted to see works on a cruise ship that comes to St. Lucia every so often. On my first vacation I was told he had just left two days ago, but I was much luckier this time. He was the one I thought about when I was thinking about opening up my video rental place. The old crew loved old-school karate and after every karate show we saw, he was the one I used to try out all the moves on, or vice versa. We eventually met and talked about old times and new times, and that was it. People change and I could feel the difference between us, as we both said "I'll see you later" and went our own ways. It was not like it used to be. But I was still happy to see my old friend and know that the struggles of life didn't defeat him.

After reminiscing about my boyhood days, I walked to my store, where young and seductive were waiting on me. People on the islands believe if someone comes from America. that person has to have money, the U.S. green. And something else I learned through experience is that the women come after me just like the guys go after the new fling on the block.

167

Chapter Fifteen
Hottest Chick

I remember a family moved into our area with two daughters when I was growing up, and all the guys and I tried to be the first one to get close to one of them. I tried and tried to get close to the young one, but my game, my confidence, and my beauty were not my strong points.

But on the second night of my first vacation I met her and we joked about growing up and how I tried to get some from her. With that same laughter she invited me to her house, but my ways have changed so much so I turned her down. After our conversation, I left and thought about it.

My wife is so far away from me and there is no one on this island who knows my wife. I couldn't get a kiss from her when we were growing up, but because of America I could be served like a king.

It took awhile before it dawned on me why all those girls were coming around my grandmother's house , a place I used to chill out in. I always thought that they came to check out their friend, my niece, but they really came to check me out. Now I had become that hot chick on the block wanted, and they were after me to see who could get me first.

This one is sixteen and filled up in all the right places, and this one just turned eighteen and every morning I see her, she is pushing her chess on me while we talk and suggesting I could have those anytime. This one has her man who comes to my place, and she tries the hardest to be the first one. She would go out of her way to make sure I noticed her, and if a hot song was playing she would make sure I was looking and then make an extra special seduction move so she could get a reaction out of me.

I sometimes think about it and my thoughts always end up on her man, my friend, the one who helped me out every morning. *Why do I have to have a conscience now, when it is so easy to do my dirt so far away from my wife? But what if I did have sex with her? Could I still talk to her man the same way we always do, or should I keep my mouth shut and enjoy the ride?*

The night of my birthday I received a birthday gift from a seventeen-year-old but I turned it down. One of the guys gave me the key to his house and the seventeen-year-old was willing to give herself too me as my birthday gift to rip open however I wanted.

Two for the price of one. It is most men's fantasy. In my store one day while I was talking to one young lady who wanted to be the first to have sex with me, another one joined in on the conversation and our talk quickly turned into a double dinner date. Both of them looked good and one of them already told me a man could make a woman do anything. I never had it so good before: all those chicks just for me. Young ones, young ones, and not so young ones, and so far I picked none but my wife, and she was so far away.

Now the ugly duckling is getting offers left and right but he is not responding. I wonder what all those women are saying about me as I spend so many foolish nights alone, hugging my many pillows and listening to the rain making love to the galvanized roof.

"What's up/" I said to young, tender Roni.

"I came for the thing," she said to me.

"What thing?" I joked back to her.

She is fourteen and dresses in a very revealing way, and there is something in my store she wants but she does not have the money to pay for it. Thoughts went through my head as we walked into my store together, but at the same time I was frightened to be alone with someone who was willing to brush up against me for something she just has to have.

It didn't take me long to turn around and head back outside store where everyone could see nothing was going on. I do not trust her and I do not trust myself. It's been a long time away from my other half and my feelings are very strong. I try to avoid the young, tender Roni as much as I can, but she keeps on inviting me to some cookout. I thought the whole situation through, regardless of how sick it may have sounded, but I thank God for my new conscience now.

I am grown man with a grown sexual mentality. Sleeping with Roni would be nothing but molestation. *Why would you think about something like that?* my little voice said to me. *If you want to think about something, think about this: Supposing a grown man bribed your young daughter into bed. Wait a minute. I was not thinking all that. Okay, so stop thinking what you are thinking.*

For some reason the item she wanted from the store would not sell, and she kept on bugging me for it. So one day I made a deal with her because she visits the country every weekend. Certain foods I couldn't get in my town, but in the country they were plentiful and so she brought me all the fruits I ask her for   and I give her the item that she wanted so desperately.

"Sister Brown, would you like to braid my hair for me? I am paying."

"Why not?" she said.

So we sat in my videogame room and let the braiding begin. She is one of the few women I could talk to without the conversation turning into the topic of sex.

"So what's up?" I said. She tells me about the situation she is going through with her church. She is a Christian and I am a believer, so we have something to talk about besides sex, and that is where I get all my pleasure and happiness from.

It was a pleasure for me to wake up in the morning and not have to go to work on time. It was my pleasure to build a swing for my nephew and his friends so I could push them higher and higher. It's always a great pleasure for me to see the rainbow over the sea so early in the morning while I am jogging , and it always makes me think about Noah. It's also a pleasure for father and son enjoy to the same house without argument , I experience that. It's always a great pleasure for me to enjoy the waterfalls and the birds in the background singing to me as I lay my head on a giant river rock, enjoying the sun. It's my greater pleasure to sit in my tree so early every morning reading the Lord's book. It was a pleasure to hear sister Brown humming some Christian song while doing my hair. And at the same time she was telling me about how her church kicked her out because she is not married to her live-in boyfriend.

I could hear the love that she had for her church and the sadness in her voice about being kicked out. I told her that Jesus Christ is Lord and that always brought a smile to her face and mine also. She was surprised to hear I knew so much about the Lord and I tried to follow his words. I also told her I love Jesus and my wife, so I try to stay faithful to the ones who have my back.

Chapter Sixteen
Out of Disaster

Out of nowhere here comes her boyfriend running into my store, passing me and coming right back out. He tapped me on the shoulder. "Come here, come here," he said to me very anxiously. "I want to show you something." By the way he was acting I knew this was nothing but trouble. He opened up a bag and goose bumps took over my whole body, and that was not the only time I had had uncontrollable goose bumps ,so let me tell you about the second story.

My life in New York is supported by being a construction worker. I help build skyscrapers. But this construction day was like no other day in history, as my wife called me frantically, telling me a plane had just crashed into the World Trade Center, and while she was in disbelief the second one hit.

"Honey, honey get out of the city," she yelled at me. "It's a terrorist attack." I couldn't believe what she was telling me as my cell phone went dead on us. My job was not too far from the World Trade Center, and then I started seeing big black smoke rising to the sky. Not long after I could hear the fire trucks, police cars, and ambulances all speeding down the West Side Highway, so the whole construction crew rushed to the streets to see if this could be true.

"Oh boy. I can't believe what I am looking at. And everyone else around me couldn't believe it either. I could actually see one tower burning but I could not see the other one. Goose bumps took over my body and my skin turned cold.

"Yo! Where did you get this from?" I said as my eyes opened wide to see a twenty-pound bag of cocaine in his bag.

"In the backyard, buried in some foreigner's house I was working on." he said.

I had never seen so much cocaine before, so I was shaking because I could see a whole lot of trouble coming. He said there was a whole lot more cocaine so he was going back to get more. The following week I left sweet St- Lucia so I do not know the end of that cocaine story, but I will continue my 9-11 story.

Goose bumps would not leave my body alone as I stood on the West Side Highway looking at the scene. I am looking right at it but it does not look like it is really happening. More fire trucks, more police cars, and more ambulances are speeding down the West Side Highway. Now I can see people coming out of the disaster area with black faces.

Black people, white people, and people of all races are coming out covered up with dust and ashes. I stood there staring and staring and staring, and the moment I turned around the second tower came tumbling down. Everyone on that highway yelled out, "Oh my God. Oh my Lord."

Out of disaster comes togetherness, and out of togetherness comes caring and sharing. That day race didn't matter, life did. I saw small stores and big businesses giving out water and hugs to anyone who had tears in their eyes, so the whole city was embracing one another. Everyone was trying to get out of the city, but every exit was on lockdown so we were basically stuck in the city.

People were asking officers how they could get home, and finally one officer said, "The Williamsburg Bridge is open for pedestrians only. So that is where almost the whole city and I were heading. From the Williamsburg Bridge you could see the thick black smoke drowning that whole part whole of the city and every one on that Bridge is in disbelief. If only I could get to use one of those public telephones so I could tell my wife I was coming home, but every phone had a very long, long line of people waiting to call their loved ones.

That is why I am so excited to write about my vacation. September 11 changed the whole world. On that horrific day we all did the same things we usually do, get up in the morning to face another day of hard life. Passengers on that plane and some people in the World Trade Center were probably procrastinating about taking a dream vacation or thinking about making a change and doing something they always wanted to do in life. It was like a story I know about an old West Indian man who came to America to make a better living.

So he worked all his life and never took time out to enjoy the money he had worked so hard for. He said to himself, "When I retire I will go back to my island to build a house and enjoy the rest of my life in peace." So at the age of sixty-five, he took all of his money and went back to the island to build that dream house that he had sacrificed so long for.

But one day while putting the finishing touches on the roof, he suddenly had a heart attack and died right on his roof. He never got the chance to enjoy life or live in his dream house. Tomorrow is promised to no one and no one knows when it will be their time, so my sympathy goes out to everyone who lost a loved one on that day. Don't let fear stop you from living.

Now that the world is in turmoil, I am still planning for my retirement but at the same time enjoying the road to retirement, so if I do not get there at least I got to enjoy some of my hard-earned money, instead of someone else who didn't work one day in their life for it. So life is sweet when you know where to look for it. So can you tell me if this next story is true or not.

Chapter Seventeen
True or False

I meet a man who found something during his search for his destiny: the way to a good life. So he tried to encourage me on my days of frustration in a world that gets more and more frustrating. Deep down in him he told me there is a voice that from the time he could remember telling him to find his destiny. But he never listened to it and kept going on his own and living the way he knew how to live. Year after year and confusion after confusion in his life, that voice kept on telling him, "Find your destiny and you will find life."

Everyone has a destiny in life, something they have to do. There is something you know you have to do, but you can't figure out what it is. That's what destiny is all about: looking for what you are good at. That is what he told me.

He said ,i have listened to too many men and friends telling me the right and wrong things about life, but all their advice couldn't help me to find my destiny. Only the voice he wouldn't listen to knows him and we all have one in us that we don't listen to. Until life got too hard for him, so he cried out loud from his soul. The part of you that never dies. It just goes back to the one that made it and then all those questions start: What did you do with the life I gave you? Why did you never take the time out to find out? Where did you get life from? Who was the one who put good things on the roads of people's destinies?

"My destiny was preplanned for me," he said to me. "A road map was put in me to find my calling and many adversaries were put on my road to try to hinder my many achievements. Two worlds were created. One is a testing ground and the other is the reward for passing your test.

"Pain and suffering will be a thing of the past and families will all be one. On my journey," he continued on, "I never actually met anyone but the souls of people looking for their way home or an easy way out. I couldn't tell one race from the other and soon realized they were all made the same. The only difference was in their behavior, the way they acted toward some other soul pushing their way through, trying to get their reward.

"Where all they stress will be replaced with rest. Where hate could never step up to love, and love will always say, I love you."

"Why find rest," one soul said to him, "when you can just stay here and frighten the ones who are looking for rest?" Let's make them lose hope, take away their courage, and tell them no one will give them rest and there is no reward for good souls. So abandon your foolish idea of finding your destiny and join us in our one life to live, because when you die it's all over.

No one travels that small and narrow road because it is long and difficult, so we stop here and cause trouble for those who are willing to try it, like you. My calling is to travel that road. The cost doesn't matter. My soul must be trained to listen to the one who calls it home, the place I must deliver my precious cargo.

There will be no excuse or explanation that I can give if I fail my only mission. Bring my soul home safe. I meet brothers and sisters who made it home and by their example I know it can be done and must be done. Their ways of life have inspired me to keep looking for the things that were put on my road to help me battle the evil spirits, who know that I know that the road map is correct.

One soul brother, who I met on my journey that inspired me to take that tiny road, showed me all he had because of his faith and belief in the one who had called him. "All good souls can hear some voice calling them to seek out their destiny, and I came from the least of my family to become a leader of many families," the soul brother said. I am put in the right place at the right time to help those who get weak on their journey to find the one I found.

I was introduced to many strong and powerful souls from the old days who were stupid and foolish enough to seek out that small road that leads them to riches and happiness. I am the king of souls, so I know my souls and my souls know me. The souls that follow me will be rich beyond their wildest dreams and honor will be added to their honorable souls.

How could I stop looking for the life that was preplanned for me to enjoy? But my faith let doubt get in the way. The one I know said to me, as I listened to his strong story about what would happen to the souls that do not make it home safe. Good souls are rewarded for the chance they took to find out if it is true or not. Corrupted souls are also rewarded for trying to prevent the good souls from reaching their place of rest.

"I have a mansion of my own beyond the sky," he told me, "and you could have one too, only if you stay on your road. Every soul road is a little bit different and every soul has a reward waiting for them, regardless if they find it or not. Don't try to follow the next soul's road or else disaster is waiting for you for trying to steal another soul's destiny.

Corrupted souls are all along the journey, waiting to corrupt the ones they can corrupt, but they can only frustrate the souls that are following the voice they have heard since their youth. One bright soul is always watching to see if his souls are getting weary on their journey to meet the one soul that gave all souls courage. "I could see," he said, "all things that take place on that road, and I could name every soul by its name. No soul could hide from me, and no soul can lie to me, the one who knows all thing and gives all good things to those that seek him.

Protection is what I give to my souls who find pleasure in searching for me. My souls were shown things that other souls will never see or know, just so I could keep hope alive in them. I have called many to this journey, but few souls will be chosen.

The corrupted souls and the ones that are always trying to stop the other souls from getting there will be punished beyond what their souls can even imagine. This is what he said to the corrupted souls. You have your own journey but you steadily try to stop my souls from coming to me. You are always putting obstacles in their way to make them stumble and fall, but I am good to them, so they might stumble but will never fall.

I will always be their crutch and I will always keep an eye out for them, but ask for the tray layers, who just don't have a clue about what's going on, on this road of destiny. Pain, confusion, and frustration will be those souls' reward. Torment is a good friend of frustration, so it will be added pain, something like judgment, where souls will be separated into two groups, the achievers and the disobedient ones.

"Souls never die," he told me again and again, "but they can feel joy and pain, love and hate." His story continues, "On my journey I saw souls who couldn't take the pressure and fell to the wayside. Some fall in pits, too blind to see their way home. Others just plainly give up, so none of them will be called achievers.

No souls coming home are supposed to complain about his journey, because every trial makes it stronger for the next trial and no destiny is easy. Don't forget souls never die," he always keeps on saying as he tries to make me believe his story. From the moment I passed trials and tribulations, I decided to go all the way and many good things came my way.

A soul that makes it home and gets its rest is greeted with loud songs of joy for having faith when all hope was gone. Halfway into his journey, he started getting offers from temptation, tempting him to join his in his way of life, but he said "never."

When I am weak is when I want to be strong, and when I am strong is when I thank the voice I always know. That's why the soul that makes it home gets such a loud standing ovation.

Before my soul gets its long-awaited rest, it will get to move around and show all the things that will be his and answer all those questions that always bug the soul. I was also shown what happened to the corrupted souls—the ones who have sold their souls for profit—but my eyes and ears couldn't bare their punishment.

Now that my soul is home, it will be put in a room and guarded by two magnificent souls in their rightful place of quietness. Do you believe my story?" he asked me.

"I do not know," I replied, "but I will think about it."

"Don't forget," he told me again, "souls don't die. They just go back to the one that made them."

Chapter Eighteen
Hi, Honey I Am Home

"Hi, honey. I am home." She didn't know I was coming and I told no one but my father. Two days before I left my beautiful island of St. Lucia (a.k.a. just simply beautiful) where I learned the color of a business man (money green), I told everyone that I was going to the country to spend a couple of days with my brother, so I would be closed for a couple of days.

I tried to give away a few things to my close friends but didn't want it to look too suspicious that I was leaving the island. I gave a couple of my CDs to the guy who played music for the area, and I gave away the reggae CD that I played every night, which always kept the night crowd mellow. Especially Sister Nadean who always came running when ever she heard this one particular song.

It did not matter what she was doing. Whenever that song was playing, she was out front, moving to the best songs of Crow's nest. My partner in crime was the one who always helped me out, the one who would do anything I asked him without hesitation. He was someone I could count on whenever I called.

I thought about what I could leave my partner in crime without him being suspicious about me leaving, so I told him to come to my store and pick out some of things that could still sell. After the backpack was filled with stuff, he left to see how much money he could make. That afternoon he returned with almost everything and told me he'd had a bad day; he'd only made a small amount.

I kept everything in the backpack and took it to my father's house and told him and my father the same story. "Dad," I said, "in two days my friend will be coming here for something. Give him this backpack and tell him it is my gift to him." I told my partner to go to my father's house in two days and help him cut the grass.

All the change I had left over I stuffed into a small pocket and I gave the bag to my paps. At twelve o'clock I packed my small suitcase into my big suitcase and headed to the airport. One person saw me with the suitcase, so I told him the same story: "I am going to the country for a couple of days."

I took a transport that passes close to the airport and told the driver I would pay him ten dollars more if he made a small detour to the airport. You know I sat by the window, rested my elbow on the window ledge, and rested my chin in the palm of my hand to let that country air hit me in the face one more time.

The driver did what I asked of him, so I gave him what I promised. I checked in and had some time to kill, so I walked to a refreshment stand away from the airport and had one more taste of St. Lucia red snapper with rice and peas and a nice cold St. Lucia beer as I sat under some big pine trees smiling about the chance I took on myself.

My plane touched ground, so I checked myself in. At the check-in line, the woman who inspected my luggage asked me where all my clothes were. She said she had never seen anyone travel with empty suitcases before. I told her I had left all my personal stuff at my father's house and the clothes on my back were the same clothes I wore when I came to St.

Lucia, so I was leaving the same way. I know I will be back and my same washrag will be waiting on me.

I took my window seat and watched the beautiful blue water under the plane's wing until we disappeared into the thick white clouds. I'd like to thank my readers for hanging with me, and I hope I did help you in some way. Tell your friends about this book.

I also hope I made you laugh and think about your own life, and remember a vacation is good for the mind. I am going to build a guest house on the island one day, so when you come to sweet St. Lucia you could drop by and talk to me face to face. Or you could stay at my guest house and I will tell you something like this: Love is a gift to the world, so it sees no color.

My wife was happy and surprised to see me and my spirits were back up for a while. Just like a good movie, at the ending we made sweet "I miss you" love throughout the night and fell asleep happily ever after. Goodbye.

About the Author

He was born on the beautiful island of St. Lucia and came to America with his mommy in his teenage years. He soon realized that life is filled with trials and tribulations, so he had his errors and failures and needed to learn the right way— is the best way. He has only one goal in writing this book: to show that the human mind is the greatest power we all have. Think about how the richest man got rich—whether he got his the right way or the fast way. Also think about the men who escaped from Alcatraz. They all found a way to get what they were after by using their minds.

P.S. Buy my book and exercise your mind.

Printed in the United States
108691LV00005B/40/A